BREATH BETTER SPENT

BREATH
BETTER
SPENT

LIVING BLACK GIRLHOOD

DaMaris B. Hill

BLOOMSBURY PUBLISHING

NEW YORK • LONDON • OXFORD • NEW DELHI • SYDNEY

BLOOMSBURY PUBLISHING
Bloomsbury Publishing Inc.
1385 Broadway, New York, NY 10018, USA

BLOOMSBURY, BLOOMSBURY PUBLISHING,
and the Diana logo are trademarks of
Bloomsbury Publishing Plc

First published in the United States 2022

ISBN: HB: 978-1-63557-647-4; EBOOK: 978-1-63557-662-7

Library of Congress Cataloging-in-Publication Data is available

2 4 6 8 10 9 7 5 3 1

Designed and typeset by Sara E. Stemen
Printed and bound in the U.S.A.

To find out more about our authors and books visit www.bloomsbury.com and sign up for our newsletters.

Bloomsbury books may be purchased for business or promotional use. For information on bulk purchases please contact Macmillan Corporate and Premium Sales Department at specialmarkets@macmillan.com.

to the generations and the futures.

Years ago, she had told her girl self to wait for her in the looking glass.

—ZORA NEALE HURSTON, *Their Eyes Were Watching God*

CONTENTS

PREFACE
Breath Better Spent: Living...

At this moment, I am a writer who lives and works a teaching job in Lexington, Kentucky. This is a place that has little love for the me and the Black girl self I carry on my shoulders. These feelings have intensified since the murder of Breonna Taylor and the subsequent attempts to smother public outcry regarding her murder (such as the political attacks against Attica Scott that criminalized her professional responsibilities as a legislator). When I speak of love, I speak of community and a type of nurturing environment that allows my writer self and my Black girl self to live uninhibited. Any love that is available to me in Lexington, outside of the Black women writers/artists and allies community, is often conditional and in many cases a kind of love that is transactional. The love in this city is given as a type of reward. I never have the courage to forget that the love and affections I do experience here are akin to some type of radish, rhubarb, and pumpkin-spice jelly love, like lye in with your chocolate love. And I like my love sugarcaned, honey-dipped, and fluorescent, a neon advertisement kind of love, billboard-style love and big enough to read when you are way down the highway and told to you in many tongues, told in two or three different languages kind of love. A love like water veining the earth, even in the concrete spaces, until the rubble runs out and the water blankets her like an ocean kind of love.

Love and nurturing are essential parts of the human experience. A secure foundation of love and nurturing bears many gifts; imagination might be the greatest of them. Our desire to know is like the smell of the first mother's neck and the ways it winds into her girlhood story. We want to know everything and what was human before we left the nests of Eden with a sack of water from the Nile. Modern civilization is far from Eden; it has chosen other priorities and untrustworthy scribes. So I will begin here, not in the imagination, but in the "knowing." I am a remnant of what used to be known as an "American." Likewise, my writing is cloaked in the intellectual and creative legacies of American literature, but what inhabits my writing cannot be discussed outside of the context of my Black girlhood experience in this place we call "America." In this book, I am telling you a story illustrated in pieces of my heart and fragments from my mirror.

This book may be some long-forgotten promise. "Years ago," after I freed myself from some of the expectations this "America" had for me, I told my girl self, the one who waited to greet me in the looking glass, that I would bring her with me. I promised that I wouldn't stuff her, my girl self, into my girdles and the other undergarments that make me fit for the world we live in. I promised to carry my girl self on my shoulders and celebrate her. In this way, I am acknowledging the ways she has been a warrior and protector of my sanity.

Many of the pieces in this book are semi-autobiographical. In *Black Girlhood Celebration: Toward A Hip-Hop Feminist Pedagogy*, Ruth Nicole Brown defines Black girlhood as "the representation, memories and lived experiences of being in a body marked as youthful, Black and female." With this theory in mind and my girl self on my shoulders, I have named this book *Breath Better Spent: Living Black Girlhood*. The conceptions of breath are central to this book. Every breath in physical or sacred form, every laugh sounding like a giggle or thunder, every whispered joke or secret—even the currency of gossip—every prayer I utter or the prayers uttered for me, every gasp, every praise and squeal were sound investments, good time spent in girlhood. Take it in. Breath is both individual and profoundly communal—particularly in the form of language. Breath is a type of life force. One that is both physical and spiritual.

The title includes breath because it takes in the experiences of Black girlhood, not in isolation, but in conversation with what we understand to be life on this planet at this time. These poems examine the cyclical lives of Black girlhood that does not confine itself to age or geography. It also takes special care to talk about recent Black girlhood experiences that I have encountered in my "womanhood," like my time spent with Saving Our Lives, Hear Our Truths (SOLHOT), a volunteer collective that celebrates, respects, and honors Black girlhood, and Black Girl Genius Week, a public showing-off of SOLHOT epistemologies and values. My time with SOLHOT is best articulated by my sister poet Nikky Finney. She describes the experience as being "in the tradition of the old Camp Meeting Revival, where the longed for spirit makes the journey to be fed and *is* fed."[1] She also reminds us that "SOLHOT is in the ancient tradition of Black women and girls creating sacred space."

Another experience that continues to empower and sustain my Black girlhood is my time with the Urban Bush Women (UBW). UBW is a performance (dance theater) ensemble. I spent time with the ensemble at UBW's Summer Leadership Institute (UBWSLI) in New Orleans, "a ten-day intensive that serves as the foundation for all of UBW's community engagement

---

1. Nikky Finney, "Foreword: Pinky Swear: SOLHOT & Dr. Ruth Nicole Brown, Pioneer," in *Black Girlhood Celebration: Toward a Hip-Hop Feminist Pedagogy* (New York: Peter Lang, 2009), xxii.

activities."[2] The intensive begins with an examination of the self, because we collectively understand—as Audre Lorde and others have taught us—that in a society that is patriarchal, a place where oppression is expected, normalized, and encouraged in many ways, caring for the self, particularly if you are youthful and/or woman/womyn and/or Black and/or differently abled and/or poor rather than wealthy, is a political act. From there, the UBWSLI teaches us to imagine the world differently and then strategically be the difference we envision. And when we have finished that, it is our job to ignite the change we envision. This type of workshop takes you to the center of your being. The center of my being begins with an examination of Black girlhood.

In kind, this book lives beyond my personal experiences, within a collective Black girlhood. I was born in the Appalachian mountains, not too far from Lexington, Kentucky, in Charleston, West Virginia. I was grown and nursed in the concrete tributaries of New Jersey, one sweet hour from Philadelphia. When I returned to the area a few years ago on sabbatical, I spent many days visiting The Colored Girls Museum in Germantown, Philadelphia, and its genius founder and director, Vashti DuBois. The museum is "a memoir museum, which honors the stories, experiences, and history of ordinary Colored Girls."[3] The museum asks, "Who is The Colored Girl?" and answers, "She is of the African Diaspora." The Colored Girls Museum is sacred art space where the objects nourish me. Many of them rely on African diasporic knowledge and art-making that is

2. Urban Bush Women, "Summer Leadership Institute," accessed July 2, 2021, https://www.urbanbushwomen.org/summer-leadership.

3. The Colored Girls Museum, "About Us," accessed July 2, 2021, http://thecoloredgirlsmuseum.com/about-2.

described as mixed media and/or pastiche. These poems are a type of ekphrasis inspired by an exhibition there, *In Search of The Colored Girl*, and the mysterious disappearances of Black girls—reflecting a kind of meditation on Black girlhood and detailing some of the realities of Black girlhood in contemporary American culture and global context.

In addition to the aforementioned, the meditations, poems, and work included in this book recognize a 2015 report by the African American Policy Forum and the Center for Intersectionality and Social Policy Studies at Columbia Law School titled *Black Girls Matter: Pushed Out, Overpoliced, and Underprotected*, which encourages us to protect the creativity and freedom that Black girls cultivate. The report also illustrates where we as a society are failing to actively love and protect Black girls. How, as a result, we are collectively fostering an American society that makes Black girls particularly vulnerable to being incarcerated within their lifetimes. For example, the report states that Black girls make up 16 percent of the girl students in school settings, but they are the demographic that makes up half of school-related arrests. The report reminds us that examining these suspension rates in American schools is important considering the connections between them and the pseudoscience of "superpredators" among school-age students acting as the driving force for legislators to support the militarization of school discipline—even though this crime wave associated with "superpredator" students never materialized.[4]

---

4. Carroll Bogert and LynNell Hancock, "The Media Myth That Demonized a Generation of Black Youth," The Marshall Project in partnership with NBC News, November 20, 2020, https://www.themarshallproject .org/2020/11/20/superpredator-the-media-myth-that-demonized-a -generation-of-black-youth.

Monique W. Morris illustrates even more glaring connections between public schools and the juvenile justice system in her book *Pushout*, finding that Black girls are the fastest-growing population in the juvenile justice system.

———

What does the active love and protection of Black girls look like in "America" and in a time when extreme oppression and violence is stimulated? I do not pretend to know the answers to this. What I know is some patchwork and remix of stories, inclinations, and experiences of Black girlhood. Stories are the treasures I own. They are what belongs to me. I once heard a story about a Black girl on a plantation in Washington County, North Carolina, the one next to the sixteen thousand acres of water that make up Lake Phelps, that brushes up against Somerset Place. There, there was a Black girl who labored on the plantation, in an enslaved capacity. One of the three overseers left her in the stockade overnight in the winter. Despite the belief that winters are mild in North Carolina, they can get quite cold; she was stricken with frostbite while being punished in the stocks. The frostbite was so intense that her feet had to be amputated by a doctor on the plantation. A few days later, one of the three overseers, probably the one who had sentenced the Black girl to the stockade, was poisoned. There isn't any proof that the overseer was murdered by anyone at Somerset Place, nor do I advocate for murder in any circumstance or situation. I value human life above all else.

When the enslaved people on the plantation were questioned about who poisoned the overseer, the oldest Black man there confessed, most likely to keep others from being unjustly punished. The authorities did not believe him. Then the second eldest on the plantation, probably a grandmother, confessed to the poisoning and welcomed the punishments that the other overseers and the local patrolmen offered. Likewise, they did not believe her. Before the questioning was over, an entire family, kin in one way or another to the frostbitten Black girl, was accused of the crime.

The entire family was thrown in the local jail and threatened with death. Their offense was actively loving and defending a Black girl in a time of extreme social oppression, inequality, and violence. When this family was imprisoned, Josiah Collins, the man who owned the Somerset Plantation and by extension this family's physical bodies by law, was sent repeated messages by the jailers, telling him how they couldn't shut the family up. They were sitting behind bars singing a glorious song of the people. It went "Jimmy crack corn and I don't care / Jimmy crack corn and I don't care / Jimmy crack corn and I don't care..." They sang for days. What was not said in these messages was how the jailers dared not whip, maim, or kill this family of Black people who were intent on protecting a Black girl. What was not said was how long this family sat in jail knowing they were worth more alive than dead because of their enslaved social status. All the while they remained vigilant in their knowing, knowing that the Black girl's life and freedoms were worth more than the whole lot of overseers, jailers, and onlookers. This family continued to mock the jailers with their singing. Ultimately, this family that had fiercely defended Black girlhood was not killed, as many had wished; instead they were sold to plantations farther away in the South. We don't know if members of this family remained enslaved or emancipated themselves. I mean, without the comforts of family and the infectious laughter of Black girls in your ear like music, why stay? Why call a place without the laughter of Black girls in your ear like music "home"?

In unrelated events, in a body that shares genetic code and blood with those Black girls previously enslaved on Somerset Plantation, hundreds of years after the previous Black girlhood story was archived, I share roundtables with a small group of Black girls at the Wild Fig Books and Coffee bookstore in Lexington, Kentucky. It is 2018 and this bookstore, named for the brilliance of Gayl Jones and her poem "Wild Figs and Secret Places," is owned by an immensely talented writer, Crystal Wilkinson. Crystal and her granddaughter Leanna are among us, but Crystal is in the corner with her coffee and pencils, writing stories. We, this group of Black girls, with names that are Christian, Muslim, and original, are crowded around tables, sitting in the light of books that shield us from the venom of the world. We are writing our stories together, weaving our lives, using pens as some type of loom and computers as some type of time-machine technology. We are thinking on what is "Ours" and what our desires are in this time and space, because we believe in the power of bell hooks and her writing. Auntie bell hooks tells us that "knowing what you want is the first step toward power." And we all believe in her and in the power of desire. Anna K. Stone is writing our collective Black girl writer story in a million photo clicks and hundreds of videos. When she is not doing that, she is interviewing us about what it means to be a girl in this time and place some call "America."

We are there, writing together, telling our stories, and benefitting from grant money aimed at amplifying the voices of Black girls and young women of color. We call our writers' workshop that centers on our voices, Black girls' voices, and young women of color's voices "Giggles, Guts, and Glitter." This workshop allows us to create autobiographical stories using twenty-first-century artistic practices associated with literature, remix, and pastiche. We say we are learning to read and write. What we are doing includes building community, becoming family, reclaiming space in a neighborhood where gentrification is encroaching upon all that Black girls see and love. We are writing this and remembering to breathe deeply and laugh often. We are telling one another that our ideas and desires are valuable. We are roll calling the names of Black women writers in Kentucky and beyond. We are strategizing about how to be fearless in our love for one another and our communities. We are actively loving ourselves and writing various recipes for how to stay free.

I run drills; I ask these Black girls for their opinion ALWAYS. I want them to articulate their desires at rapid speed. I ask their opinion always so that they are and will be ready to lead. We lead and serve one another without shaming or investing in hierarchies.

This book, like life, is cyclical and a kind of Sankofa, a kind of return, to the Black girl self that knows and loves me deeply—nurtured by the range of emotions, knowledge, and experiences of Black girlhood, some of which I mentioned previously. I need to remember this self, remember the self that survived the 1980s and 1990s, a time of greed, excess, and perverse poverty, a time when girls were the caviar of more powerful and often wealthy men who have been the embodiment of success and have modeled the expectations of modern American masculinity.

Breath Better Spent: Living Black Girlhood extends from the collective "knowing" of Black girlhood culture. These poems explore the public and interior lives of Black girls—the visible, institutional spaces, like schools, and invisible spaces, like the home or the imagination, that Black girls occupy in American culture. This book is divided into three parts and two decimals; they dangle like sequins. The opening section, "Black Girl Genius," explores histories of the Black girl geniuses. It discusses their exceptional abilities within the context of ordinary living. It is punctuated by an essay, "Only Boys Have Fans," that explores dreaming and being in the context of Black girlhood. The second section, "Twice-Born Girl," is a remix. The semi-autobiographical poems include samples and crosscuttings of my Black girlhood experiences. I include them because I value the Black girl self that I carry on my shoulders. She is radiant and resilient. I know that she can help me answer broader and more complex questions, like how do Black girls understand desire and power when threats of hypersexualized visibility and stereotypical presumptions are ever looming? This section is followed by "Gristle," an essay that details how external forces disrupt and destabilize Black girlhood.

The final section of the book is entitled "In Search of The Colored Girl" and was inspired by the exhibit at The Colored Girls Museum that bears the same name. These poems primarily focus on the disappearances of Black girls within the United States and their communities. This portion of the book also considers some ideas about Black girlhood in a global context, particularly the #BringBackOurGirls movement. #BringBackOurGirls was an international movement comprised of advocates for the 276 girls kidnapped in April 2014 from a school in the town of Chibok in the Borno State of Nigeria. To date 112 of the girls are still missing. There are additional religious and gendered tensions embedded within this conflict.

Hoe work (1940). Photo by Dorothea Lange. New York Public Library Digital Collections.

They add layers and complexities to the kidnapping of these Black girls within the context of human rights issues and international relations. Therefore, the poems in this portion of the book explore the complexities of Black girlhood in the context of nationhood, empire, and what is considered diplomacy.

In *Breath Better Spent: Living Black Girlhood*, I am asking you to hoist up your humanness, particularly that portion of yourself that connects to your youthful self. And during this activity, you may encounter the Black girl on my shoulders. If you are very lucky and more human, we may invite you to journey with us.

* * *

Your first grown-up job
is to keep a secret about
dead people among us. It
beams from you like a torch,
a thorn-studded fruit tree fenced in
barbed wire. If you live in America,
ghosts blossom in dollars. They will
tell you "you smell like a Haitian,
revolution, taste like ground glass
in gravy."

Your secret is a caress on the bottom
of the mourner's bench. Your secret
is a splinter in a pew; it's a heavy
clap. Your secret's voice is a technology
that carries over, collecting a woman
humming, juggling her eyelids. Knowing.
On an unclaimed holiday you roam, lost
to the crossroads. Your heart beats, a hymn
runs like a frog in your throat. A wino calls
you "banshee," brushing the earth out of his ear.

BREATH BETTER SPENT

BLACK GIRL GENIUS THE HISTORIES

Group of Phillis Wheatley Girls (circa 1922).

New York Public Library Digital Collections.

SPEAKING IN TONGUES
(for Phillis Wheatley)

It ain't how they tell it. P-Dub, you were not
born half-grown from the belly of a ship
bearing the same name. The hue of your skin
is in the same shades of cedar and mahogany.
Planks are not evidence. The bill of sale is no
birth certificate.

Your first name is as old as a giggle and lengthy.
Nedjma, a star. Aiza, the cleaver. Your name stenciled
in Sanskrit and Aramaic tongues, written in a book,
one that engraves dynasties. Your father called you
music. He couldn't keep you from scoring melodies
across his palace walls. Your grandmother was
throned—chewing on rods of honey, knighted
you a scribe, commanded you to be about
the business of wonder. Silence, the first
alarm. Your auntie went blind when she heard
that you had been stolen. Sand blistered
her skin. It's the salt gash above her eye.

In this Western wilderness, Greek words are grit
in Anglican dialects. In English, Latin reads like
a wart in your eye. Gaelic phrases sound like bones
breaking. Language is a sore that quivers, cursing
a cleric's lip. Grace can only be found in the slant
of ink and the quill on the side of your eye.

JARENA LEE: A PLATYPUS IN A PETTICOAT

Smch, God knows that woman? Jarena Lee,
righteousness, lightning flooding into ears.
Your mama calls it early. "You got a mouth
on you." Your prayers like brackish, whirling
echoes, your mouth is a river that won't lie
still. The old woman at the dock warns,
"I smell gills under your collar." Men say
your feet too big for you to be a lady.
You got feet like Elijah, the kind with wings.
The men snarl and snort like the messenger
Hermes done left a wish list in their nostrils.

You are womanish when your sermons
spill from your mouth like rugs laid on
streets of gold. Holy men will boast, name
you Paul, and wish to leave you limp
at the hip. You are known to have good sense
and a better swagger. You the woman with feet
like fins on Jonah's whale, and a greater mouth,
carrying God's word like two fish and five ladles'
worth of drinking gourd. You look like a platypus
in a garden to the bishops. They say you
a spectacle, a sideshow doo-wopping behind
the wood of the cross. Curse you. Jealousy seeks
to cleave you, dividing the living in two. Church
mothers smocked in white will whisper "watch her,
Rev. Jarena Lee, like that Jacob, wrestling
a pulpit out the paws of stingy angels."

Little Blanche Taylor, Franklin, Kentucky, age nine, fourth grade (1907).

BELOVED WEIRDO

You are not digging this book
about a slave girl and her
incidents. The pages read
about her early knowing
of all things, meanwhile you
know you ain't got a stitch
of sense. If you did, you
would have put that book
down and hit that boy,
asking you if your name is
Beloved and if you are gonna
be like Sethe and kill
the newborn baby he wants
to put in you. Is he the weirdo,
watching in on you and your
bestie leaving the women's
clinic?

You wish you would have
gone wild as the wind on him
for prying. Instead, you go deaf
and dumb thinking on it. Your
mind wanders into a book. You
think on asking Miz Harriet Jacobs,
how does a girl learn to be a slave?
Does a snake bite you and leak

Only known formal portrait of Harriet Jacobs (1894). C. M. Gilbert Studios.

venom until you fall cripple
and spasm, zombie you into
a slave? If no, then you gotta
swallow a butterfly and let it
flutter in your throat, smother
your words until you become
a slave? Do you let the butterfly
kick you way up into your tonsils?
This might make your eyes rummage
the floor for cracks and force you
to be humble. Can a slave be made
from a butterfly that avoids the windows,
avoids light? Does that butterfly become
a bat under a girl's collar? Or do you crawl
under the hoof of a horse named Andrew
Jackson to become a slave? The horse
galloping and neighing at your earlobes,
dirt in with the blood. To be a slave would you
have to take your ribs and fashion
Andrew Jackson's hooves with ivory shoes?
Would the overseers use your teeth
to tether, hold Andrew Jackson's shoes
in, like nails? In the cradle of your Black
wringing neck, do you offer the nag
a pedestal and curtsy at the mare's
master? Just curious, not dying
to know.

THE BIRTH OF MA
(for Ma Rainey to Rainey's Black Bottom)

You shimmied out of your mama,
onto the opera stage.
You shimmied out of your mama arms wide,
hollering Vaudeville.
Your kindergarten classroom is a late
afternoon cabaret.
You sashed and skipped the whip, corn husking,
and cotton.

The daybreak of Zion quaking in your jaws.
Muddy Georgia caked on your lips. The snake
charmer in your mouth, a scaled mystery keeping
company with saltwater eels and freshwater gators.
Your lilt is thunder, chopping hellbroth
into laughter. Your blind nana said she smelled it
in your pamper. You are a song's elixir.

Dance, Cake Walk (1903). Photo by ulstein bild via Getty Images.

Children of defense worker, Negro slum district, Norfolk, Virginia, 1940.

Photo by John Vachon. New York Public Library Digital Collections.

ELLA BAKER AT THE BALLOT

Some young girls sing all
the words in your mama's blues
records for half nickels. The Morning
Star is at his kora—crooning, begging
you to sing in the voice of Memphis,
like the Mississippi, like the sky
is crying. This serpent is wooing you
to holla behind the sweat that insists on
hurrying after him, like smoked paprika
in his mammy's peach cobbler.

You tell the devil that you read like lightning
and you better with letters. You figure
you can't find arithmetic enough
to keep you from the ballot. You and
Fannie Lou got evil scurrying out of corners
and courthouses.

"NEVER GROW OLD"
(for Aretha Franklin)

You said "Never Grow Old" and swore
you wouldn't. This disco is church-
happy, stirring joy between your knees.
Your worries disappear into the bop. They
rock steady, far from your responsibilities.
Huck Finn ain't the only one to know fun.
Ben Franklin nibbled at what he knew about
how to grow better. Meanwhile, your voice is
caramel, lush, wet and warm star-kissed
sugar around everyone's soul. Their hearts
bare, naked as a baby, bathing on
the dance floor. A piano churns, you
coo, your eyes floating behind smoke
liners. It never grows old.

African American girls playing games (1922).

New York Public Library Digital Collections.

Narada Michael Walden, Aretha Franklin, and Whitney Houston recording the song "It Isn't, It Wasn't, It Ain't Never Gonna Be" (1989).

Photo by Michael Ochs Archives/Getty Images.

SOMEONE FOR ME

Only a queen has soul enough to tell
you how Whitney walks backward out
of a tar barrel of secrets, stained in sequins
and cerulean. She knows your mamma
favors her own. Women with the same
eyes, full of storms, sorrow, the winds of
change swelling in their cheeks. Raised
in church, your mother and hers are
like double mirrors in a powder room,
tarnished against the wall, smudged with
misery. Her mother, your mother…nothing
could please them. Her mother, your mother
plead for you to "tuft it [lust] into a wedding"
mattress. Your best friend, a robin, is perched
on your wing. Clive Davis grins, grabs you
at the shoulder and dresses you in prom queen
drag. He tells Arista Records to spell your name
p.o.p.s.t.a.r. A chorus line of "the kidz" springs
from his limp wrist. You are his Barbie doll molded
from the riots of the '60s. Her mother, your mother
know he's talking jive. The churchy mothers,
the magi, the sacred sisters of Aretha Franklin
see the second coming in you, a blues woman
swaddled in silks.

ONLY BOYS HAVE FANS

When I learn to love North Carolina, it is an Olympic year, 1984, and we run, we race. We suck wind in through our noses and out through our mouths. She is eight and I am ten. We are obsessed with our blooming breasts, but in this moment, we do not worry about looking flat-chested. Like little birds, we want to show our ballooning ribcages. Running is all we know. We are from the Carolinas where the beach cuts into the marshes that are stitched into the forests by fire ants and a whole world of predators. Running is the way.

We circle our grandparents' front porch. My cousin, Brandi, and I are ringing around red-and-rust-colored tiles and the steps are paved green with plastic turf. We are Florence Griffith Joyner and Jackie Joyner-Kersee. My cousin is wearing her signature bun and bangs. Her face is a hue of honey; it makes her look Asian to some strangers. My skin is a shimmering cinnamon when lotioned. No one thinks that I am anything, other than a Black girl. I have a puffy ponytail that is always wiggling out of barrettes. My cousin's kid body is toned with muscles and I wear my pudgy belly like a badge of honor. She has gapped teeth and mine are wildly crooked, but we wear our smiles like trophies. Because we imagine that we look like Flo-Jo and Jackie.

You can see it in our bond. We jump from either end of the porch, hurling sticky bushes and vaulting saplings into a cushion of pine needles. We cheer for each other. We are girls and we learn

In honor of Black History Month, espnW runs a weekly personal essay about the influence of Black female athletes. Adapted from DaMaris B. Hill, "Only Boys Have Fans: Growing Up Racing Like Flo-Jo," espnW, February 4, 2016, http://espn.go.com/espnw/voices /article/14715131/only-boys-fans-growing-racing-florence-griffith-joyner.

early in our family what everybody knows, that only boys have fans. Until we can convince others to believe in us, we believe in them. I lace up in Flo-Jo's motto, "Dress good to look good. Look good to feel good. And feel good to run fast." We race fueled by giggles, uniformed in fluorescent colors and golden glitter nails. My cousin is always the better athlete. I am running behind her and cheering for the athlete of the century. She is set to win it all, when I do the unthinkable.

I crash into the cement. Bam-bam. Slipping on the turf-paved steps, and worse, like a girl, I cry. My cousin runs to aid me. She forfeits her victory, like most women do, to take care of family. She cleans my injuries with kisses. This is something we see our mothers do. We are girls, we understand that chasing beauty hurts a bit. She promises me that this is a small thing and I believe her. We are generations. We are champions.

When I left North Carolina that summer, I cried lakes and lashes because I loved her. And any distance farther than fingers between cousins is too far. We wished family forever. I blew kisses and waved to her through the rearview of my daddy's cranberry-colored Cadillac.

By the time Flo-Jo returns to the 1988 Olympics, I am fourteen. My nails are long, nearly six inches in my dreams. My hair is big, and I have ambitions of being a writer. I stuff draft poems in my training bra. I am smart and have learned the reward system that skirts beauty. But I am also young and unsure how to be strong. I do not know how to run in heels, but I still wear them. I want my legs to be long and lean like Flo-Jo's, the legs that win her four medals that year, three gold and a silver.

It made me sad to learn that everyone is not like my cousin; some people are mean enough to bully butterflies. It hurt to hear them say that Flo-Jo's win was wind-assisted. I say her victory was in the prayer she whispered. Let the record stand. The fastest woman in the world was Black, beautiful, and fortified in her faith.

TWICE-BORN GIRL

Aretha Franklin recording her album *This Girl's in Love with You* at Atlantic Studios (1969). Photo by Stephen Paley/Michael Ochs Archives/Getty Images.

WHAT YOU TALKING 'BOUT

Like the dead-seeming, cold rocks, I have memories within that
came out of the material that went to make me.

—ZORA NEALE HURSTON, *Dust Tracks on a Road*

1.
you scary all the time
you live in a world that don't never make sense
you haven't learned the currency of lies
you got honesty scabbed on your lips
you got scars on your face
you got worries, hot and blistered fright
you figure truth must taste like poison
you got a mother. she got love and hate in breast milk
you got a daddy. he got stank breath and itchy kisses
you got anger like inky oceans, spills and rages
you ain't got enough paper
you swallow whole notebooks
you sneeze, you make glue
you got two baby sisters who think you are their mother
you clumsy, scrapes, bruises
you know cliffs, not boundaries,
you can't count good or measure love
you got decimals down
you real good at long division and remembering to forget
~~you~~ everything down to the milliliter.

2.

you don't think you are pretty
you think hips got power, but you missing them
you got sisters who are your best friends
you got a god, one who listens
you know if it weren't for fictive cousins…
you'd be frayed at the edges and long dead
you will know one man. he is fine
you don't know he will burn the sight from your eyes
you are his next woman one day after school
you will kiss him deep
you will not have the words when he reaches for
you, the scars clawing after
you for the rest of your life.

3.

you will love again
you will love a man who will want to cage you
you will carry this man's son
you will be a girl, a mother, a wonder
you believe wandering is a kind of love
you will spend the rest of your life running
you will become an abolitionist and never stop being a girl
your love will be the greatest power you know
your love, she will confuse and awe you
you will embrace love with a long-handled spoon
you will pick through love's flesh for fish bones
you tell yourself, you will not choke or die for love
you are afraid to believe this.

Aretha Franklin recording "The Weight" at Atlantic Studios (1969).

Photo by Michael Ochs Archives/Getty Images.

Aretha Franklin dancing for the cameras (1968).

Photo by Express Newspapers/Getty Images.

4.

living is a lot like love.

living runs with lit matches

living burns all caution from you

living tells you Sade is grown folk music

living knows Aretha Franklin is ether

longing got teeny ears

living say "Ms. Franklin sings too hard on me."

living is something that can only compare to an uncle
        squeezing your knee

living say "she sing to me like I have to want to survive it"

living is an ever-infant Earth in you, spinning toward the sun

living got her voice pounding 'cross your temples

living got vocal light pouring into the black universe of your
        heart

living putting thunder in your arteries

living is the press of the shadow on your neck

living ain't little and scary. she stands in the yet to be known.

5.

you girl, cry out, wail, be heard,
you hurt if you got to—then
you get on with it...the living
you better laugh, wrap your arms around a love that frightens
        you
you hold love like you a whale fluttering beneath him. no,
you be like an octopus feeding. there is a man
you love. he will hunt you in his days and dream of
you for 30 years. he will taste
you in the rhythms of his sweat. call out for
you whenever he shuts his eyes—because
you are a dusty gypsy with scars like hieroglyphs
you call tattoos.
you have made men itch in places that are a mystery to them
you will be the candy dish of a nation's fears.

6.

you will hate black jelly beans and
you will touch boys and think love is licorice.
you will say it is toxic, and hear your mother call it medicine
you will take more sugar than your kidneys can handle
you will pee every time you ride on the handlebars of
your neighbor's bike, no kid will call
you pissy, they will know you by your smell
your whole world will be a prickly thing
your mother's lap will be a thorn bush—
your secrets will make your best friend bleed from her eyes,
you know from the scratches at her wrists.
you will have a wailing that will enter kinfolk like a siren
you will love Ms. Franklin and call for her guidance when
your knees are flat from praying.

Aretha Franklin holds a copy of her *Soul '69* album at Atlantic Studios (1969). Photo by Michael Ochs Archives/Getty Images.

7.

you never imagine that no one but your best lover will call
you witch. you will not want to know why
you will cover your ears when he fusses
you will remember your first prayers
you will remember a sitter recording your baby voice,
you, your prayers for hostages on an eight-track
you two will remember the prayers being answered
you, your words, on the nightly news in the mouth of Walter
        Cronkite
you will know the power of the tongue
you will be an unmarked cassette tape and stuffed between
        your mattresses
you will want to be a boom box, because you don't know better
you will yell in frustration. They will lie, tell
you they can't hear you, ask you to whisper, scream
you will run, and it won't be fast enough
you will jump, and it won't be high enough
you will dance off beat, because you hear across time
you will want tornados to give you breath
you will make demands of earth. concrete will forsake gravity
        and scrape
you at your ankles. It will want to cut like diamonds at your
        thighs.

8.

Black girl, all of this will want to carve you,

Black girl, do not hollow your heart

Black girl, make room for a melody and shimmy

Black girl, with your ragged teeth, chip out some space for a
    lamp in your throat

Black girl, torched by the sacred voice of Ms. Aretha Franklin,
    you,

Black girl, carry only your load and do not grow weary of your
    heap

Black girl of hope and sorrow, your voice is a burning bush

Black girl, ignite every rock of fear in your belly. They always
    telling you,

Black girl, to be a lady, but no one prepares you to be a woman.

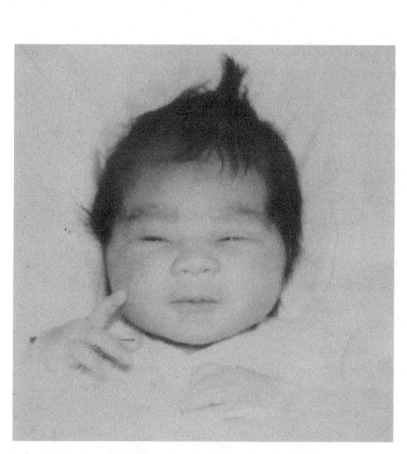

Infant. Photo courtesy of the author.

GLUTTON

Three and a half weeks past
the calendar's bullseye, refusing
Earth and entry. You feed. Your mother's
body can't keep. It shrivels. You burrow
from her a prickled pixie. 5 lb., 12 oz.
Hungry. Ettling her breasts, hosing
her for milk until dawn and over
again. Staring into the sun. You need. No bib.
Nothing misses the lips. Nothing is enough.

Sore and withering, your mother pleads.
Doctors prescribe steak, to feed
your flesh. Ox pulp coddles in your
coos. Your gums are scavengers
for fur. You tear into and from. Your father,
familiar with curses, counts the goose bumps
coating your belly. All know you are
afflicted. Perverted to your pores. Touch
and tongue, two ways to taste. Born
desire, a glutton, in a world of war and
fiends. You twist toy soldiers in your tongue;
the doll straddling high chairs.

THOSE SUNLESS SUMMER MORNINGS
(for Winton McKinley Hill Jr.)

Summer mornings too, he rose
from the jungles of dreams and starry skies
with cracked hands, blistering mounds of service
stitching all that ached. Camouflaged
in decades of workdays and war in France/Korea/
Germany/Vietnam. They made him a modern
man of ritual, spangled a legacy out of every day.

You are born two long lifetimes too late, ignorant
to the arts of love and war. He is deference,
black dye at his graying temples, oatmeal clumped
in his printed news. You are the cursory granddaughter.
You make white hairs furrow in his brows. You
will grow to be a woman who embraces explosives,
gets over lovers quickly, remembering he survived
land mines and surrenders to four granddaughters,
up to his boots in barrettes and Barbies.

What is home without me? (1914). New York Public Library Digital Collections.

HOTTER THAN JULY

You sit on two clouds of bees, honey
storms in place of your hips. Your waist
is an underripe watermelon, a tense
and tight drum. You carry daisies for breasts,
with dandelion eyes. Summer is skipping
away. Every radio humming static. Electric
is July. Hotter than we remember, which
is why you pray for her return, carrying sweet
onions in the hot grease of your armpits, salt
and soda crackers in the creases of your neck.
July is the 7-Eleven of your childhood, fluorescent.
Your jelly sandals are neon. Your panties—
washboard and starch white, snapping
hand game rhythms with your belly
button. The driveway is your playground
littered with Christie dolls and cordless curlers.

In the attic, you play with your vanity. You
pretend it is a crib. You skip circles around
a stool, sit on the top of it, Blue Magic hair
goo on the back of wrists. You pick at a face
mirror. You blow on it to reveal the musings
of your mustache. You karate kick an ankle
into the air. Flash freeze. There. You tiptoe
balance between chipped toenail polish and
your need for October. Middle school is a

A young girl with braids and blue barrettes laughs with wide eyes while shopping in the South Side of Chicago, Illinois, 1973.

Photo via Smith Collection/Gado/Getty Images.

distant dinner guest. It is July and you are still
a girl. You wrestle back the pink folds of your
body, cuss God for holding the woman in you
for ransom. You beg for the blood. You want it,
rushing, shiny, thick and lush like your hair. Enough
to uppercut yourself in the tum. Blood enough
to inspire envy. You want it lava-hot and licorice-
sweet. You want the boys to tell you that you smell
like rusting quarters. Rumor has it that a girl's
first blood is chocolate. You want it enough to chew
Big Red when chomping on Cocoa Puffs and Pop
Rocks. You want blood enough to make friends
with the witches among ordinary women. You run
relays to the store for these "hussies." They drink
ice-cold Pepsi without staining their laundry, always
hanging their rusty drawers dashed between the sheets.

Whitney Houston as a senior in high school, during one of her first professional photo sessions (1982). Photo by Jack Mitchell/Getty Images.

SIGN O' THE TIMES

You know much about VCRs? Heard that boy
from *The Last Dragon* is with Whitney? Every
boy on your block is in love with Vanity, dying
to be Bruce Leroy, a juicy warrior, gilded like
Jermaine Jackson from jheri curl to jawline.
They train with karate flicks. On the news, Reagan
says cities be damned, the Blacks are frozen in time,
but Jesse Jackson got his finger on fast-forward,
shouting *believe it, achieve it* from outside the shot.

You are confused, out of the loop, behind the latch
of the tape. Your life is slow motion. You are swaying
in Elmer's glue between good girl and what you think is
grown. Your Black girl words are harmonies sampled
under the electric cords of mics and braggarts. Your
breasts, coned, sip cups stuffed into something supportive
and silkened. Why press rewind? Replay it all? To be
the scratch in the groove of disco. To be the girl
on the beat and in the breaks? Jesse says Black folk are
winning. Blinded by the Times, Ronald Reagan is Sho'nuff.
Black and ever after runs like a commercial, sliding
into Carefree curl. Your afro pick banished like the glow.
Your community is no longer golden. It is frostbit in
your fists. Your president is a master at disaster, sends
military planes to hand out poison and pistols in place of
progress.

GRACE FOR BE'LA DONA

you all drunk in rhythms,
swaying sinners' praises.
your riffs ripe with fury,
you winding junk for yards,
lucid and lingering
you united
churchin' it.

god's morning star
knows no minstrels.
you are a belle,
a brown sugar baby,
got the devil in ya.
let your smile tell it.

god bless the talker
that know how to jelly roll,
can call them to be baptized
in your syrup and sweat.
go-go cover your soul
leave all funktified
and without regrets.

go-go, you-you,
d.c.'s afro-beat, blues boo.
go-go, grab Gabriel

hit 'em over the head with his harp.
go-go, chuck Joshua.
the best horns are all vanity 'til
go-go, blow 'em back.
djembe voiced and voodooed
go-go, gather in your prayers,
liftin' your legs in pure elegance.

the pocket. ain't got.
no stairs from hell
to heaven.
you backyard and basement.
you experience the unlimited.
you rare in your essence.
you go-go, grinding
spirits in your organs.

"Don't Mute D.C."—girls dance on a police car on 14th and U streets in Washington, D.C., at a protest in solidarity of supporting go-go music and D.C. culture. Photo by Kyna Uwaeme.

DODGE CITY GIRLS
(for the sisters waiting in the wind)

dope never stayed downtown.
you can't fence what is damned
and dusted. it floats. uptown is
fluffy with daddy's girls in goose-feather
down coats. good girls are born greedy
for something gritty on their lips. good
girls are green. big sisters are giddy on
ganja when they glide around the way.

in school they tell you gravity is
science. no one says to you that it is
as simple as love. no one explains
the symmetry, so when you follow
a trail of cotton candy that snakes
into an alley slick with satin pillows,
no one can convince you about danger,
plush concrete. you have to feel it, burn
in your throat, the lust for winter, bitter
confections between your gums. Nancy
Reagan says "just say no" and you read
the hollow faces of sisters who dance
Swan Lake for the taste. frost.

STILL SCARY

fraid of bugs, babies, popped balloons, sticky
peppermints, cracks that would break your mother's
back, words that sound like windows breaking—your
heart is too fragile. Fright over voices that are pretty
enough to ride rafters, lyrics that climb on ladders.
Afraid that a piano chord is a stairway. You scared
of spiders and the ole saints frying chicken in church
basements, smacking on bacon with crackling rinds
in the pews. You timid 'bout every boy you ever adored
and never told. You hiding from happy. You terrified
of joy. Them two got heartbreak on the horizons.

Infatuation is an affliction like bedbugs, creeping
in like seventh grade thirty-five years later. You
squinting and giddy. You drooling at the luster
and past lives in his shaved head? You ain't
never had good sense. You ain't never know
the difference between curiosity and chaos. He
got you cheesing. Each of his cavities carries
a cavern of stories you want to know. You tell him
to gift wrap his wounds, serve them to you on a broken
plate. This is a trap, an illusion, a way to convince him
you are brave. Watch him watch you gulp all
his demons and everything that scares him. You
are a woman and have done it all before.

When you are eight, you follow a pack of boys
into the woods to find a vine. These boys are swinging
Tarzans, banging their caged hearts, tempting violent
deaths. You celebrate each boy's victory. Faithfully
forget your ride across the wild. Your eyes closed.
Your heart open and abandoned. You did not fall
or break your arm. You didn't take a second turn.
Refuse to ride in the back of wagons. Every page
carries wood, paper cuts, and toe prints, marking
the spot you gripped before the jump.

Self-portrait (2021). Photo courtesy of the author.

HOW THE TONGUE HOLDS
(an Incident)

his tongue is covered in twenty-four shades of fur.
he howls compliments,
plucks you from a pack.
maybe you are fit to be one of them,
the kind of girl who glitters,
a glamorized gargoyle
of high school legend?

the Fates are older, sixteen.
they wear pomegranate lips
their words are bank notes and myth,
"he is King Midas. Paints
everything money green."
his gold-plated tires
take the face of black licorice
in a wedding plate.

his high-rise apartment
windows surge sun rays.
he is radiant. You are pressed,
a shapeshifter, tinsel,
electric sweat in his
palms. Your protests—
a scratched 45
tugged on a turntable.

You don't remember music.
Your age is one candle more
than a dozen, still seven short of
a score, and he is a man. he has
two rulers' worth of tongue
and a second scepter for conjure.
there is only one way to say no
and you are too young to lie.

SAGE POETS AND POPSTARS

Miz Brooks keeps an eye on you *In the Mecca*. Her ear
to the streets, eyebrow perched like a limb, "if you ask
a question, you must keep going. You can't stop there.
World will waive: will be facetious." You fly off the
handle. Giggle and grab dictionaries. Point straight
through the *f*'s. Thump the definition when you
eye it. Curious through to the core, you
leave the library with questions in your walkman,
"How Will I Know"? Finger fluffing your bangs,
make them wiggy. You and Whitney wondering,
 what is really love? You kissed a couple boys
and their cousins. Left fruity-sweet lips on the necks
of them, in choir closets, on baseball fields,
and in staircases. You write love letters religiously
to other girls' boyfriends. They are recipes,
love spells. You say little. Three-way calling...
is mischief. The person on the other end,
the jinn.

Whitney has the voice of rainbows
and hums glitter, how could she feel weak? She
tells you falling in love is bittersweet. Crab apples
ripe, foul, and reckless in the arches of your feet.
Cicadas sing long-distance through phone lines.
The lightning bugs are out the jars, flying about
the kitchen. Love comes in SweeTARTS, batty

boyz finger poppin' in passion's doors, affections
in Easter colors. They love like mood lipstick.
Laughter is lust you share. They switch, hold
hands with bookworms, blow kisses through
beauty shop windows, skip when they see
mirrors, and other mysteries.

A young Whitney Houston beneath a poster of her mother, in her bed-room in West Orange, New Jersey, circa 1982. Photo by Bette Marshall/Getty Images.

Girl reserves (1919). New York Public Library Digital Collections.

CONTINUOUS FIRE
(a love poem for a younger self)

Little Wonder, your heels be steady.
They plant lightning in the Earth.
This is one way you hum.
Your song is a peace that cracks concrete.
The vibration is a nectar that heals.

Little Wonder, slow your marching.
I am running swiftly behind,
attempting to catch up, with my arms
extended, my breath trying to lock
in your hair. I am desperate to
reach you. My toenails are flaking.
I am falling from my flesh. The lava
of my veins gushes.

Little Wonder, your heart and fists,
they are pendulums. They swing,
pumping toward heaven, propelling
past and post-present. I am too
slow to even catch a glimpse
of your wrists. Is that where
you keep your wings? They are
a blur at this pace.

Little Wonder, curious and confused,
water cheerleader wannabe,
may I fashion you a throne?
May I carry you on my shoulders
as I praise you with my pen?
Make a drum of my head.
In our first and second spirit tongues,
tell me the stories that stretch the holes
of history. Teach me how to call the
forgotten names. Crisscross your ankles
before my heart. Your arches resting round
my breast, I will rub the calluses
from your feet with my hair. Dry them
with my lashes in bursts of worship.

IN THE WILDERNESS

You follow four strangers, a lantern,
and a cousin into the darkness, across
the threshold of a wood cabin owned
by daddy long legs. These spiders
are landlords that won't leave you be,
these black acrobats, crowded in every corner,
all eight bunk beds and four window frames.
To mark your territory, you shake your soft
bedding, wait for the boom. You smuggled
a radio in the bottom of your duffle bag.

The technology of sound is as ancient
as flights to freedom. Acoustophoresis
is the power to levitate objects with sound.
No textbooks required. You are the children
of holy rollers, proficient in ritual. Begin
with three Mystery Mix flavor Now and
Laters. Break the bodies of flashlights. Spill
batteries into the floor. You know the science
of sand. Read one another's palms for fortune.
Use the forbidden arts to resurrect what is left
in another life. Pop each battery in ass of the
boom. Aroused by the smell of sweat, static
and concrete in the cassette tape. The one praying
presses PLAY. The button sticks like watermelon
Bubblicious in the base. Levitation begins. You

are back spinning in the cabin, loose like fallen
leaves. Your long legs form a lanyard of splits.
Rise to become robot. Pop lock, snake dance, wap
and fold into the floor like a centipede. You
are worshipped for this.

Unless you are the one who is Dizzy in the ear,
always Bird in the runs of notes. On the lookout
for the ole saints trying to capture your soul. You
know them when you see them, wearing skirts
over their jeans. Their hands deep in sweaters, warm
like feather beds. Their tongues serving sharp ice.
You signal a warning, B-girls and Anansies pose
as if at the altar. Spirituals trail into the wild.

WASTING HER LIPS

1.
You can't keep a secret or stay in the yard. If love
is like the wind, you are loose like water, a gossip,
a woman only in tongue, and you claim Kiki for
a little sister. She is a year younger than you
and all you know about love, you tell her.

"Love is greedy. Do you want him? His girlfriend
is just a thing in the way. He is someone a girlfriend
is about to lose. Dive into the cracks of doubt, tap on
the fractures of his feelings. Be the backspin of his
ambition." Kiki asks, like jacks? "Like pick-up sticks,

like slaps in hand games. Keep up with him." You and
Kiki are always together like sweat and jelly bracelets. You
are sponge rollers and powder pink. You are pre-debutante,
wishing to be bridesmaids, ironing velvet letters into cotton
T-shirts. You are grape lip gloss on top of cherry Blow Pops.

No one is sure if you are sisters or twinning. Everyone in
Jersey is talking about Whitney Houston and her ways.
Your teeth are crisscrossed. Hers are bucked. You're fat-
cheeked dolls in the face, but got Barbie's hips puckering
out of your pockets. Your boyfriend will remind you of this.

Queen Latifah and Monie Love backstage at the Genesis Convention Center (1990). Photo by Raymond Boyd/Getty Images.

2.

Your boyfriend is the boyfriend wooing Kiki, your
sister-friend, in the streetlights. You can see them.
Under the porch light, dim as a confessional. You
are being courted by a grown yet young man. He
keeps clearing his throat, says the older sista next door

thinks he is the father of her daughter, an ugly baby
with eczema and anger in her face. This man's mouth
is a poorly built bridge. He thinks his tongue is a sacred
heart. Pointing at his other girlfriend's car, the one he drove
to see you. Bragging on buying it. Asking you about
your favorite color. Candy apple or Jolly Rancher green?
You can't stop talking about this book you wished you were
reading. Tell him you might change your name to Sula. He calls
you a good girl. By his math, this makes you worthy, better than
the girl with the car and the older sista, staring from her
       window.

She with her ugly baby that is your suitor's mirror. At 14, you
think men and money grow on trees. Pomegranates sprout
in your pores, you taste blood in your mouth and are not the
       least
bit worried. You have crutches in your closet for times like this,
twisting your ankle chasing confessions. "Safer to feed
       squirrels
from a spoon," the older sista is warning. She wasting her lips.

BORN AGAIN AND AGAIN

(for Edith Walker-Lowe)

[*Premonition*]

My father's life will be a jigsaw puzzle, double-eared and
irregular pieces, a portrait of a man your father will never admit
he knows. Your father will push away from the table. The perfume of
Jezebels will howl in his robes. Your father will abandon his vows. Your
father's congregation will hiss, coil around him, and sting him in two dialects.

[*Opening Scene*]

I am three the first time I die. Your flesh is a cleft between
the dashboard and car floor. Glass and concrete are pebbling
in your freckles. Your grandmother will leave paradise, spill oceans,
and frack mountains to get to you. The doctors will see her levitating
in hospital lighting. You will wave to her from the darkness.

[How the Body Functions]

Resurrection is not painless. The eyes will land first, doing the work
of the heart, because your eyes have more muscle. Your tongue
is languid, the last to make it back and most divine. She is the strongest
muscle you know, because you have a twin-grandmother tongue,
one like the one you witnessed overthrow antiquity.

[Scenes at the Grave]

Speaking of the Africans who can fly, ask Hester Prynne about
the "lick of tar" at her wrist. Ask Tituba of Salem, "What can she spell?"
Ask Baby Suggs to preach the sermon about how Beloved found her
way in this world. Your woman tongue can hoist bodies into heaven,
when it dances from the margin of the brook, taking her old place.

[*Foreshadowing*]

For years my father will have faith in the armor of manhood
and fornicate with the idea of being human. Your father will abandon his
family a little bit every day and for longer spells in the evening. Your
father will swear he is working. It is darkest when your daddy ain't
home. It will be midnight when you realize that your father is unholy.

[*The Arc of Miracles*]

My grandmother begged for my life, not miracles. Your grandmother
is an itinerant god when she raises you from the dead. So what,
if your hips arrive before your knees? Spend the life she gave you
tucking your left hip bone into the socket of your liver. Your kidneys
will be hourglass stacked and your lungs will be cupped into your forearm.

[*Imagery*]

The roof of my mouth is a tabernacle of polished jewels, but your tongue has an affinity for strays. She calls for the long dead. Sees them fading in and out of living room armchairs. Or they are the ghosts that live in your "Human Nature" poster. Or the haints that mime your name from your reflection in the mirror. Being born again ain't easy.

[*Opening Dialogue*]

"At three, your daughter is dead." The words puzzle your father. An EKG machine eulogizes you in Morse code. Your ventilator plays a funeral march in A-fib rhythms. The second time you are born, you have no navel, no fur, no veil. You break your mother's tomb of expectations. You don't walk through walls. You firk from behind the door, eyes doing the work of the heart, tongue…

[*Symbolism*]

lingering. Resurrection is merciless, excruciating, like every other mystery. You wake to testify, cry in the bosom of a woman who has waited for her girlhood self in the looking glass. You witness how she force-fed, choked down love, following the drums of her grandmother's prayers, licking sweat out of the palms of demons. Combatting the weapon most men fear, the womb. First birth is war.

[*Flashback*]

The second birth is worship. Your first spirit, your grandmother, hovers over you, speaking holy tongues into death's canals, where you are the beloved orphan of the ungodly. The doctors tell her "breath is better spent on the living"; you hear your grandmother's prayers in your nostrils, because your ears are doing the work of the eyes. Your eardrums are stained in light.

[*Static Characters*]

Caged birds sing. Like Maya Angelou and so many women before you, you once sat in the children's section of the Colored Methodist Episcopal Church. It is the same procedure when you are tied to the hospital bed with bars. There are no lavender taffeta hospital gowns. They are tattered morgue sheets seamed into your wounds with bloody dressings. They smell like compost under your nails.

[*POINT OF VIEW*]

Are there instructions about how to make a father? You go to the first book you know, your family Bible. Thumb through Exodus. Ask the Jews about young fathers. Your god has a chosen people and no sons. Did your father waste forty years, two generations, in the wilderness? Moses has grandchildren and dies before Israel—more humble than any other man.

[Setting That Illuminates the Character]

Black girls have a disposition for shape shifting. Did you know that the matter-molding technology of your grandmother's prayers is genetic? Your doctor is old and untowen, cursing you with his jabber jaws, daft to the power of the tongue, the muscle that dances back and between the sides of the living. Your twin-tongue will soon be cackling about your future from the stories of what he deemed dead.

[Allegory]

My breathing is burdened by listening beyond prayer. The doctor tells your father *if* you are alive that you will never walk again. Tells him for you talking will be impossible. This doctor is a ringmaster of lies. He is not skilled in acrobatics, ignorant to the buoyancy of your Black girl legacy, the arts of adaptation. The arithmetic that rolls in your neck.

Shug Avery is finest pastor I know. She dances like she marching, her voice is a shiny trumpet on the seventh day of Jericho. She preaches every Sunday like it's jubilee, a sermon sweet with forgiveness in every song. She belches in beatitudes "helped are those who love the broken and the whole; none of their children, nor any of their ancestors, nor any of themselves shall be despised."

[Deleted Chapter]

Zora's Janie nearly died from grief when she left her grandmother's home and you didn't come back until you had buried the sudden dead. The sun sets, you will tell your best friend about it without grief. You are young and will go too quick for worries. You will leave sodden and bloated. Eyes flung wide open in judgement. The sun is gone, but you look to the footprints in the sky.

[Falling Action]

My father missed the day seminary taught about Mount Sinai. In the Old Testament, God is not always present. Your father embraces the covenant, the gift of the Torah. Your father's ten commandments are made from the marrow of the living. Your father says the laws of men are not the ways of God. Being born again is a religion of being forgiven. Cast away are the debts of sin?

[Metaphor]

My grandmother is a holy spirit. She comes to you like a mighty rushing wind. She appears before you, arms spread wide and running, waiting to embrace you. You can see the starlight in her mouth. You count each of Ezekiel's four wheels. You recall this world and the afterlife. You tumble toward her, a blazing chariot, crying out in a ring shout for power from above.

[Allusion to Theme]

I am the profit of glossolalia. The twice-born girl, the love child of Lazarus
with the skin like brick and tar. I remember when I met the Lord, spray-painted Her
face upon the Tower of Babel. Tagged our sacred names. God and I are gossiping when
She reminds the Holy Spirit that "one people speaking in one tongue makes nothing
impossible." I'm eavesdropping. My ears collect Eilat stones and angel fire.

[Resolution]

Anything you love will not leave you forever. Beloved makes the trip across the darkness,
across rivers to the shores of the living and loved. She knows the way. She's sick of waiting
in purgatory—where she sits listening to Sethe tell the story about Denver's birth too much
to forget. Beloved is gilded by the pink tongue of her grandmother, Baby Suggs, the one who kneels
down next to Beloved, the granddaughter, dead baby with her throat cut, and prays.

NEVER GROW OLD: PART TWO
(for Dr. Kim Richards, UBWSLI NoLa2014)

You are old as you will ever be,
galloping in a dance studio with an ancient girl,
ancient as redwoods and limber as Bermuda
grass. This ancient girl has shimmy style that
makes cathedrals wish for bones. Her mind
holds more mysteries than Mardi Gras. Lips
loose with comedies and confessions. She paints
them sequin, iridescent, and pearl. New Orleans
is our Auntie NoLa. Your silver-haired sister knows
NoLa's name in African and First Nations tongues.
She keeps sacred wisdom stored in her teeth.

You are a shrub, your hair is juba blanketing
your nostrils. The ancient girl can taste your lust
for cornrows in the rain. She knows the salt and
sweat at your neck is a rusting halo. She is the one
who showed you how to fling laughter from your
wrists. She transforms plastic forks into afro-pick
technologies, forms crop circles in your hair. She
begins with three parts:
create
       learn
              laugh
one is to create
       one is to learn
              one is to laugh—at will

Girls. Photo by Anna K. Stone. annakstone.com.

a girl should create

    a girl should learn

        a girl should laugh as a healing practice

you girl-create.

    you girl-learn, learn the name of every star. they are
    ancestors.

        you girl-laugh, laugh even in the face of danger.
        no one can
        harm you without your permission

create you, girl

    learn you, girl, learn all the words your mind and
    mouth can carry and command them. your tongue is a
    weapon. your throat—a cannon.

        laugh you, girl. laughter in the face of more
        powerful others is your superpower.

You are a girl. You own the power to create a world and peace
and love. Your love is the rock candy of joy crystalizing in your
blood, frosting in your breath.

    You, girl, should learn all your life, beyond your
    schooling, over the rainbow, further than the universe
    nested between your thighs, on the other side of old and
    even until the inner darkness of your navel is no longer
    a secret cell. Take the time to learn even as your skin
    flakes. She is shifting scales out of my cornrows.

        You are listening and laughing because you are
        young and nobody's fool. Too little in too many
        ways to know Aunt NoLa's sacred name, or the
        ways she formed herself from the river and the sea.
        You think it has something to do with spit, because
        your ancient sister licks her fingers and smooths
        your crown. Then you spill out into the light.

GRISTLE

Dickey Moe traveled up and down Broad Street like a clot in a vein, flaring up and exposing himself to whoever was looking. Throwing his overcoat open like an unlaced shoelace on a quick-moving roller skate, he left us undone.

We were always on the lookout for him, this Cuban man. His nose was a jumbo cashew carved into an ashy coconut. Our eyes would surf the stone and standing crowds for him. We had to walk 2.3 miles to and from school. We went out of our way to be educated, because they labeled us gifted. We were in middle school, fixin' to be women, well on our way, observant and practicing in every instance. We would be walking, watering the concrete with our sweat and switching if we saw something worth winking at. We would be the whole way through Downtown, under the tracks and Uptown in under an hour. Uptown is where we had choices, a bit of relief from our Dickey Moe duties. We could choose a way to walk and Dickey Moe, with his unshaven body, stubble on his head and chest, some of it silver, could choose another direction. We would use our words and his absence to warn him that he better choose the other.

You smelled him before he showed. Cheap wine was his aura; it lingered like the image of his large cock leaping toward you when he threw back the wicked wings of his weathered coat. We were careful to be on guard for Dickey Moe, jumping out of gray doorways or stumbling from behind bricks and buses, boasting his manhood, stiffening the spines of middle school girls. We watched for him, this villain who some had mistaken for a vagrant.

And once we passed the first pizza shop, the one that had the thick crust and water sauce, we made our way through Downtown, crossed under the tracks, used our memories and new math to count our coins. We would stop at the corner store as a reward, after we had gone on up and around Uptown and then safely into our neighborhood. This is before the solo strolls of my tree-lined street.

On the warmest days, we would take the longer way, the way that passed the law offices and courthouse. In such daylight Dickey Moe would not be near. Then we'd right our walk past Messy's apartment building. We don't know him or lust yet, so there is no need to be alarmed. Next to this building is a Catholic school, and with little worries on the last bits of our journey, we talk, like good girlfriends do—in giggles, describing all the ways we were going to get the boy we desired. Our plans are elaborate. We call his house at a certain hour and speak real sweet to his mama when she answers. Plan to stroll through his neighborhood a few days later, looking for some elusive loose candy that isn't sold Uptown. We list the people, counting on our fingers. We say the names of the people who we will interview about his likes and his associations. We are smart and will figure out the details, like which of his friends have to be distracted in order to make room for the romances we are planning, discussing and discovering what kind of kisses he will like and where he would lay them on "us." And as we giggled our whole bodies responded in a glow, even the new parts seemed to bobble. Our laughter was fragrant like bubbles from fancy dish detergent. When I feel my breast fold in like a red clown's nose and as my hands go to collect all that has deflated in this stranger's hand, I realize that I must be a freak; not only was I fluffy in every way possible, but my voice box must be stored in my breast, and when this stranger touches me, my protests evaporate like a belch.

By the time I find my screams, the kind that sail in stares, he is a whole half a block away. I want to yell at him, but my best friend, my first line of defense and only protector, shushes me. Bestie tells me to "shake it off." Tells me "it is nothing." And that "it would happen all the time and over again." Twisting my head "no," I believe her and now I wonder how she knew.

We never saw the freshly ironed Asian man cornering me in the straights of the block. He faded into the landscape, probably a lawyer. There were no warnings. Not even the stench of Dickey Moe. There was no dramatic dress coat or king-sized cock. Without those weapons, this man crooked my spine, latched on until all that was good and girl in me was gone. Made my breasts some gristle between his fingers.

Girls Too. Photo by Anna K. Stone. annakstone.com.

Outside Looking In, Mobile, Alabama, 1956. The Gordon Parks Foundation.

IN SEARCH
OF THE
COLORED GIRL

A little girl outside a grocery in Mississippi, 1996.

Photo by Shepard Sherbell/Corbis via Getty Images.

THE GYPSY GIRL GETS NO SOLITUDE
(from One Hundred Years of Solitude*)*

The poet wiggles his wrist about the first son
of Macondo. He is not an inventor. He is
a wanderer, like his mother, a spoiled boy,
a rich man's son. Colonial currency is made of
abstract and unobtainable dreams. Searching
the philosopher's stones, his mother asks, "Why
not catch God's finger in a mouse trap? The devil's
toe in a jar?" She says these things are easier.

The son never succeeds. He wears his father's
desires cloaked atop his neck. He falls into his
father's boot anxious and ashamed. He flies
the coop, from branch to tree. There he spots you,
a shiny gypsy girl. The first son of Macondo is
perched behind you in a circus crowd. His worm
warm and bricked against your back. When you step
away, he uses his beak and talons to tuck you close
to his innards. There is a moral lesson, a decapitation
on a stage. There, the first son of Macondo first enters
you, a gypsy girl. This is Thursday. Obscenities about
beauty flood your ears with ice picks.

On the Saturday, the story goes, he wraps his head
in red and anoints himself a mystic. The poet
picks his nose, tastes the man-child seasoned
in your ashes and writes. You, a smoking altar
meant to smite a son into a man.

NEVAEH ADAMS AND SHAREE BRADLEY (NEVAEH'S MOTHER)

An auntie hums "Mary, Don't You Weep."
An auntie whispers wait for me in
the looking glass and kisses the creased
news clipping. You are a missing person.
You, Nevaeh, and your mother are diamond
reflections in a fancy compact mirror. The one
the size of a sand dollar, coated in pearls or
the shape of your favorite sugar cookie.

Your mother wearing a face that is fierce
with love. Her eyes scissoring across time
and space. The demons laced you in a mountain
of landfill, like jewels staining baby diapers.

Your breath smells like the five jelly beans
you stashed in your pocket last spring. In the soft
foot of a Br'er Rabbit, sticky with the luster
and shimmer of Peeps. Your mother's back
is tufted with cascading wings. She used
them to shield you from the shards of secrets
and shadows that bloomed in Sumter like mold.

Your auntie and tribe are calling
on the guidance of the haints. They search
75 days and all through the nights, collecting
the scrap metal of dawn, shifting stories,
memories. You and your momma's images
are indigo, deep in your aunties throats.
Your aunties can taste the letters in your
name when they suck their teeth and shame
the devil. Your disappearance scorched
the sidewalk in brimstone, tinseled the street-
lights dark winter, and withered the stop
signs.

Your daddy never stopped weeping. Your
grandmama promised him she would be a
Persephone, ride his tears like a river
between the worlds of the living and the after.
Collectively, their hearts hold fifty yards of
void. And even at that distance the hide of
your murder coats the pollen and chokes.

KAMILLE "CUPCAKE" MCKINNEY

A Black girl ain't safe. In Alabama
the clergy, the crazy, and the courtier walk
into a bar and snarl about gobbling
children and hang the fangs of monsters
in stained glass windows. A felon and
his fille collect you from a yard cluttered
with balloons, birthdays, and giggles.
Dump you like last week's trash. You call
for your mother. They lodge gift wrap
in your throat. Your tonsils are callused;
your esophagus has a gas cap.

The police catalog this crime in
pictures. Not one has the gall to say
you are murdered. The scene of a
mattress speckled in blood becomes the
wallpaper of their waking moments. They
won't make a peep about it. They will
tiptoe into the same bar, telling jokes
about jackals devouring cupcakes. The
joke goes "until your nose is swollen shut
and your mouth spills screams." And the
judge slapping his knee has a pocket full
of opiates and promises for the young girl
kneeling under his dinner napkin.

Vigil for TeNiya Jones (2018). Photo by Arden Barnes.

for ALL OF BIRMINGHAM'S BABY GIRLS

our friend is named Angela Davis and you are
skipping rope. Together, you roll call
poets and philosophy, cookie recipes—
in the rhythm of double-dutch ropes and heart-
beats. You keep lists—the pens that hold
nuclear power, pencil leads that are
fashioned from Amazonian ores, the stuff
Wonder Woman wears at her wrists. You
will age bulletproof. Ask Oprah.

You do not have golden lassos the day
Birmingham is blinded by the America's
truth—no, terrorists. Americans put fifteen
sticks of dynamite into church steps, making
four saintly girls seraphs. The organ sweats
grief. The organ moans. The organ knows
the gospel of tiny geniuses. The organ
remembers when you tickled her ivory spine
with a sinner's song, "Tutti Frutti, loose
booty." The organ felt the spark you had for
Little Richard in your fingertips. The organ is
a prophet. You are practicing for *American
Bandstand*.

Your momma taught you to play piano
"with sweetness." She keeps plenty company
come Sunday afternoon. She tastes soot in
her cake batter and knows that no one plans
to show. Your momma howls, something
like Sethe, over dead daughters. And you,
you snuggle into the bench, pinch the keys
as pretty as Florentine Price to make
your momma stop sobbing over the seared
ribbon in the yard and bombs in the
bottoms of churches.

ANIAH BLANCHARD

1.
Aniah, Aretha Franklin tells me that
you will never grow old. Your bobby pin
floats in a car that has rust stains. Your
blood type dimpled into the windows.
Your car wears a wound in the roof and
a twisted smile. Your headlights are a
story. Once upon a time you wore bright blue
eyelashes. Tiffany boxes for your birthday.

2.

Every blue car on the road turns
your cousin's stomach, twists her face.
No one in your family drives highway
I-85. The mention of Montgomery makes
your cousin's memory a menace. She holds
ceremonies alone, a ritual of pinky-swear
promises, sips sugar water. She stares
into a cup of barrettes and hair beads. Makes
a list of what you shared in grade school.
To make the ritual real, she will loosen a braid
and speak your name into an electric fan. Each
collecting gravel in its waves. Clay forms on her
knee where she scraped it. Her knee remembers
you kissed it well and immediately after that
the world is twinned and speaks in code.

3.

You have few friends and there is a gang
of mongooses yipping outside your cousin's
window on the eve of Thanksgiving and
one week later, she hears that you, the only
cousin who ever mattered, one who is more
like a sister, you, Aniah, are missing. Police
howl at her to tell what she knows. She is
pointing out the window. They don't see
the mongooses' paw prints. They don't look
for predators.

4.

Aniah, your murderer's father is sixty-three
and lies, covering for a son to keep you,
a daughter, missing, and not murdered in
the eyes of the law. The trees hear his lies.
250,000 pine needles become Peeping Toms
crowding at your cousin's window. Your
cousin has time to chew each one
while waiting for your text. Your cousin
knows everything you do is an echo in her
heart.

DEAR CHRISTIANS OF ALABAMA

[*Premonition*]

Yola D's* daddy came to Birmingham because injustice
is here. A walking man like Moses, like Jesus, like Paul, Yola D's
daddy left his house like the prophets do, early in the morning,
to take his "thus saith the Lord" far beyond Atlanta to Alabama,
carrying the gospel, "good white" Christians throwing grenades.

[*Opening Scene*]

Confederate Christians are rebel yelling into the Sabbath day.
They forget to keep it holy. The Sabbath is the day a three-year-old
became an angel, a daughter became a headline gobbled between religion
and graven images of political purity. Black girls in Alabama must taste like
fruit juiced while on the vine. Are you a believer? Tell the world how . . .

---

*"Yola D" is a nickname of Yolanda King, Dr. Martin Luther King's eldest daughter.

[*How the Body Functions*]

the Confederate Christians of Alabama make Eden out of baby
sandals found in gutters and castles from cracked kiddie pools.
In Alabama there are chariots furnished in the scrap metals
of dental braces and adjustable skates. The horse carriages
drawn by jump rope. The sermons are syrupy sweet, spilling

[*Foreshadowing*]

fornication and forgiveness. Rape Black girls, gloss over the guilty,
and call your elected officials righteous. Bake layers of trazodone
into communion wafers. Use them like tranquilizers. Call the dosing
a pacifier. Are you convinced that mental paralysis is mercy for girls,
victims, blessings served from bastards to babies?

[*The Arc of Miracles*]

Confederate Christians can make you a believer? Call Alabama
the promised land, overflowing with milk and honey, where the silver
whiskers of righteous, wicked men who never forget their cravings for rust,
are the men who manufacture rivers from the metal embers of virgins'
first menses? In this land they erect marble monuments of moral law?

[*Opening Dialogue*]

In Alabama, they tell you that you are converted and convince you
that good Christian fun is as good as melted butter on your
tongue at the drive-thru. Teach you to be blind to the shaved shanks
of Black girls tossed into popcorn tubs. Expect you to be all things
grateful, willful, and ignorant. You can be all faith. Believe youth.

[*Symbolism*]

The youth pastor goes to church school and tells you the shaved
shanks of Black girls that are in the popcorn bins are not evidence.
He will tell you that what looks like Black girls is venison, seasoned
to taste, he will brag about his barbeque rub, say it is an old
biblical recipe. Holy as the one used on the Levite's concubine?

[*flashback*]

The holiest of Confederate Christians seek refuge among wicked men.
He will wink at his host's daughter and offer her his sword. Just like
here, in Alabama, just like there, in America, around the world,
the heavenly hosts of Black girls are set out on the doorposts and told
to defend themselves against the fury and feasts of seasoned Sodomites.

[static characters]

To defend themselves against the fury and feasts of seasoned Sodomites, Sunday school girls are forced into isolation. In Alabama, Black girls are endangered as brown butterflies and need protection. The coal that is pricked into the veins of marble that boasts of moral law threatens them in the voice of Roy Moore. He carries a cotton-candy-scented pistol.

[Point of View]

Roy Moore never rescued a Black girl being chopped into pieces and scattered among the monsters of any tribe. His ten commandments are a shanty tent hiding Alabama's shame. The beasts of Alabama roam in dark satin robes with lies in their fangs, boasting "'Laws of Nature and of Nature's God,' upon which our Nation began in 1776."

[Setting That Illuminates the Character]

How do Confederate Christians tend their flocks of lost daughters? Do they set them to graze and blister in the backyards of boogie men, billowing the Ten Commandments? Do daughters feed on the shrubs set under the soles of Roy Moore? You hear the whimpers of Christian daughters crying out from the wilderness of polluted landfills.

[Allegory]

Confederate Christians, where in the Ten Commandments do you take our daughters upon the mount and sacrifice them? God gave Abraham the good sense to spare Isaac and embrace the ram tussling amid the thorns. When Jacob wrestled with an angel for a blessing, he was bereft as Delilah trying to know the strength of Samson.

Civil rights leader Reverend Martin Luther King Jr. speaks with a young girl after delivering a sermon in Montgomery, Alabama, on May 13, 1956. Photo by Michael Ochs Archives / Getty Images.

[Connotation]

Engraved in cremains, it reads THOU SHALT NOT MAKE UNTO THEE ANY GRAVEN IMAGE. Black girls are your gods. Confederate Christians have turned scores of Black girls into leavened bread, sacrificing them. Politicians and open pedophiles are a roster of nonviolent offenders, wiping their juices on Judgement's robe.

[Deleted Chapter]

Yola D's grandmama has hot flashes and dreams when she is playing the organ. There she pipes on about "Never Growing Old" in the rhythm and rounds of "Ezekiel Saw the Wheel" and croons, howling Alabama is no place for Black girls. Her granddaughters are all ribbons and round as Reese's Cups at their mother's knee.

[*Falling Action*]

Rumor has it, The Moore, his teeth are coated in fool's gold. They say if he wipes himself on a girl's clothing, her futures dip into a thimble. Moore's moral laws and commandments are two Cupcakes wide and one Cupcake tall when Gov. Kay Ivey calls for chemical castration, not as a punishment, but as a protection.

[*Metaphor*]

Yola D's daddy taught her that time was neutral. Like the Bible, time— a tool to be used either destructively or constructively, like the hateful words and actions of the bad people and the appalling silence of the "good." Yola D learned from her daddy that time can be an ally for the forces of social stagnation and joy was somewhere waiting for her, because time . . .

[Resolution]

You should be asking, "What kind of extremists are you willing to be?"

On Calvary's hill, three men died. All crucified for the same crime—extremism. Two were extremists for immorality. Maybe pedophiles or men who turned the Ten Commandments into a mountain of idolatry to hide their own sins. But the other, Jesus Christ, was an extremist for love, truth, and goodness. You?

ANITRA GUNN

He wants forevers to bloom from first dates, grow
in reclined drivers' seats. His faith is in
R & B promises, and funk enough
for your uncles to smell you from the yard.
His love's stings, hornets in with your bouquet.
Your nieces will mistake flower beds for graves,

bumpers for tombstones, peach grease and gunpowder.

The odor of sanctity abounds in
the sheets of the Little boy who keeps
a collection of Barbie shoes under
his pillow. Keeps Barbies' legs in a black sock
stuffed into the battered hide of a football.
Childhood is monstrous. Ask any orphan.
Often Abandoned's house is an orchard of
bruised hearts in a quincunx of memories. There

bumpers are tombstones. Peach grease and gunpowder

are frankincense and myrrh to this deject.
Little, unloved, says scattered chocolate foils
torment minds. The barrel of his gun is coated
in the peach grease sizzling at your ear. His
tears, the wine of love lost. He tugs you into
a car bumper, squanders you in a garden.

KIMBERLY GRISHAM

The resurrection of SARS was a whisper
among the whales—you noticed the texture of water
change, between snowflake and crystal ice. You
witnessed the glass in the concrete begin to free itself
from tar graves. Startled by this rumor, your wallet leaped
from your pocket and pushed the photo of your license
into mounds. Was it there that you felt it, the grip,
shortly before you continued your journey?

Did the reach feel like reckonings of past lives...the reach
crack your vessel, exposing your heart...your heart dancing
a rumba amid winter's warning...the excitement,
evergreens carrying into the air like Christmas...lilies
blooming in the reflections of the clouds...groundwater,
did it taste like attitude...where did you drop a shoe...
your ankle intertwined with the weed in your sock...
the sock hanging over a steeple like a star on advent...girding
          us to you?

AZIYA ROBERTS #WEWALKFORHER

Five mink ferrets swaggered into Bronzeville,
snatching the seagulls eating french fries
out of their parking space at the golden arches
on 44th and MLK Drive. Everyone's

a witness to the snatching of the seagulls
eating french fries, fewer speak of the
disappearance of them girls under the golden
arches on 44th and MLK Drive. They Snap

it, stream to Instagram. Everyone is eating fries
and fewer remember Pepita or when, five years ago,
ferrets feared the golden arches and becoming stoles,
erase the disappearance of them girls from 44th and

MLK Drive. Snap it, stream to Instagram. Know
that five years ago, ferrets feared being turned into stoles.
Everything Black goes bottom-up in Bronzeville—foreclosure,
Black skin girls, penny candies, and grannies. "Good Lord."

Black is bankrupt in Bronzeville, churches in foreclosure.
The hipsters neighboring in Hyde Park stomp out their fedoras,
Penny candies and grannies have gone with the "Good Lord."
Hipsters wear coonskin caps in solidarity with ferrets. Who
        fears

the hipsters neighboring in Hyde Park stomping out fedoras?
Their hashtag #MinksRMe lit in Bronzeville marquee. Five
years
strong. Good hipsters wear coonskin caps in solidarity.
No memory of seagulls or Black girls. Ask their neighbors,

their hashtag #MinksRMe lit in a Bronzeville marquee. Five
years
since any have seen these "pigeons in from the sea."
No memory of seagulls or Black girls. Ask their neighbors,
their cobalt eyes carry diamonds. Fries fluttering from their
beaks.

Has anyone seen those girls, these "pigeons in from the sea"?
Golden french fries tumbling to and fro from the sides of beaks.
Their cobalt eyes carry diamonds. Fries fluttering from their
beaks.
Twisted, talking with their necks about the menagerie of
possibilities.

Golden french fries tumbling to and fro from the sides of beaks.
Them gulls are not cannibals. They never eat after the nuggets.
Twisted, talking with their necks about the menagerie of
possibilities.
A griot, named gringo, told the ferrets about the ways of Black
girls.
Them gulls are not cannibals. They never eat after the nuggets.
They all hand on hips, twirling necks and wrists, got the tea,
honeys.

A griot, named gringo, told the ferrets about the ways of Black
girls.
The community settled on the stoops, in the frontier of
Bronzeville.

They all hand on hips, twirling necks and wrists, got the tea,
honeys.
The treasures of Bronzeville. These Black girls are in their
Mecca.
settled in the stoops, on the frontier of Bronzeville. Careful to
avoid
ferrets and feed seagulls that flock on 44th and MLK Drive.

THE PSALM OF TENIYA JONES

"If anyone will learn my name, it is you." You knew I knew
the Black girl rules, the importance of roll calls. They are
        infallible.

If anyone will learn your name, TeNiya Jones, it should be me.
You are one who survived the Southern wilds, a Florida Black

girl running with the wind dusting your back in seawater. I am
your professor, camouflaged in the clutter of academic culture
        and

lead tongue. My mouth is a cocoon of Black girlhood, crusted
        and
caked in the corners of my mouth. *If anyone will learn your
        name,*

TeNiya Jones, it is me. Selah, and I remember you, Black girl
freckled in stars. I remember how the sun spills from you,
        selah.

If anyone will learn your name, TeNiya Jones, even in the
        lawlessness
of this ivory tower, where your style brilliance is feared,
        believed

to be feral because it roams free amid and beyond the legacy of Black

women, it is me. Selah. When *I learn your name* my mind is far from me,

shackled to the Black and tax of every professional space in America—

this is the sand in my mouth. When *I learn your name* I am the spook

that sits by the door. *I learn your name* against the grit of the King's

tongue, a space we are written and raw from the hide of half-truths and

academic knowledge. I learn your name, TeNiya Jones, the sound of it

is a pumice stone against the callus of lesser concerns. I learn your name,

TeNiya Jones, in a place where Black girls are forgotten and darkness

is the only subject of study. Selah, I learn your name, TeNiya Jones,

because I know we are the rocks in the belly of the beast, ink on the page, wight under the microscope. *I learn your name*

when I am drowning, in a crosscurrent of woman and race erasing me as I am doing the archaeology and tracing

the genealogies of our collective selves. Selah. *I learn your name*,
TeNiya
Jones, when I am the spider trapped under the goblet of the
Last Supper.

I know *your name, TeNiya Jones*, when my mind goes too far
from the shores,
Gibraltar. *I learn your name*, TeNiya Jones, when you are there
wading,

I learn your name, TeNiya Jones, because you knew my purpose
in this alabaster
Abyss. I am some buoy, some marker in this channel of
segregated intellects.

I learn to sing your name, TeNiya Jones, throughout my course
your name, TeNiya
Jones, becomes a praise song. You yodel the writing of Black
women in lyrical

cadence. *I learn to sing your name*, TeNiya Jones, when you read
every book
I ever mention. Selah. It is punctuated praise. *I sing your name*,
TeNiya Jones,

when you are ruffling across time and space, making charts and
noting dates—
details, important Black girl facts affirmed in fiction. *I sing your
name* because

you, TeNiya Jones, are dutiful in your documentary skills, each
         morsel of
formalized curiosity in your scribbling fists. *I sing your name,*
         TeNiya Jones,

when you are sun-drenched in wordplay, decoding the shade in
         Harriet Jacobs's
Incidents and the forgotten wisdom of girls and ghosts in
         Morrison. You are

beloved, selah. *I learn to sing your name* when I am a flickering
         light in a
basement classroom under a mountain of confusion, selah. *I*
         sing your name

in Kentucky, where you, TeNiya Jones, are radiant as a young
         Zora, sunbathing
in new knowledge at high noon—fiery as Zora stinging your
         eyes from a page,

selah. At wits' end, *I sing your name*, TeNiya Jones, I cheer for
         you, smile my
way back from the spaces of erased trajectories and show you
         every treasure

chest that holds a coin. I want you to see the world and you say
         "study abroad."
You are heading east, because Western wisdom fails you. Selah.
         TeNiya Jones,

you wash up on the banks of Tel Aviv, two days after two white
     girls abandoned
you in the waves. *I sing your name.* Selah. I cry rivers, I light
     candles and wait

for someone to tell me it is a nightmare. When a reporter says
     your name, TeNiya
Jones, she is a blasphemer, a woman with a lazy tongue. My
     mind flickers

like a twitching light in the basement, too far from shore to see
     the lighthouse,
or to see you standing on the shoulders of your twice-murdered
     brother, selah.

He *knew to call your name*, in the wind, selah. Your brother knew
     the Tropic
of Cancer skirts all oceans, carrying his greeting, surfing the
     shores.

HOMEROOM

Boys are restless. Charlie is batty.
Always bebop and kisses behind
the blackboard, he calls *Birdland*.
He lives below Sarah Vaughan,
says you smell like her. Sets himself
Dizzy, telling you "Miz Vaughan
sings from her pussy." His eyes
are googly. He runs his fingers
up and down, twisting his jelly roll.

You shut your eyes, cover your ears,
scatting "Misty." You sing "Funny
Valentine" to drown out Shirley
Temple's whining. You keep a jaw full
of jacks for your enemies and police deputy
Ben Fields. He spilled a Black girl
through the floor with punches.
Keep a sock full of marbles in case
he shows up round midnight.

TENDAYI'S BLUES
(for Tendayi Kuumba, UBWSLI NoLa2014)

The Urban Bush Women know
the blues be best for this mourning.
a space where lament buries
in you, long before
a blessing

Coltrane glide, cry in comfort,
these blues be best   in the mournings,
knowing if they go unsung,
these blues will rust you

Blues be best sung…
in these recent mournings.
in this women's thrall,
your soul begins to surf
Muddy Waters, licks clean
the grit that the world washed
onto your faces

Maybe the blues be best
between the mournings.
some lullaby at daybreak,
standing guard between the bullets
and your babies, between empty
nights and promises, between
your feelings and the restoration
flowing from your wells

Urban Bush Women dance company performs onstage (2018).

Photo by Hayim Heron.

* * *

you are anxious about *StarKist*,
disturbed by *Chicken of the Sea*,
neurotic as Sylvia Plath,
embodied as *Bumble Bee*,
tuna in cans frightens thee.

what to make of flesh preserved,
the threat of rust rings   drifting?
the lateral line of your canary spine,
a jaundiced memory.
tuna in cans frightens thee.

all the curves cut,
a never-ending razor rim,
shards of iron frost splash
when flipping tops open.
you might spill over.
the scars at your wrist
still itch.
nothing fits
without clinging.

every dream is a lesson.
last night,
you rocked in a wood bed
with sisters and splinters

shoved between flesh and ship's rib.
there are forty or more feet
with shackled, shaved ankles,
bone   white and wet.
you flop like fish on board.

You are returning to the beginning
where you first learned to love windows
that sting—
rain, seas, and suns.

they be better than he who guards you,
the one who says he is starved for the meat
of mermaids.
your shoulders shred
in his salt rock kisses.

your sister is born veiled and wise.
her nose leaks a salve for your wounds.
a sister that shares. she stares
and believes in ghosts.
she whispers that ancestors
crowd in the oils of your eyes.
she is waning for rescue.
she hums a visceral harmony
that carries in the rhythm of the waves.
You are frightened for tuna in cans.
horrified they may drown
in the Atlantic, aghast.
they have been dragged a-c-r-o-s-s o-c-e-a-n-s,

netted,   maybe noosed?
fit to be gobbled, englut,
in the belly of a hull.
skin, shiny black and scaled.
feet, limber like fins.
you be schooled here, this
blood-splattered wilderness,
shifting soil like tides.

BAITING BOYS

You are mother. You are a girl and four
years old the day you learn to swim.

Your father, a carpenter and a fisher
of men, like God's holy son, lays

you on a board and sets you on the waves.
You are baptized in wonder. You believe

the wood to be the plank of Noah's Ark.
You grow to believe a small thing can alter

destiny. The plank is removed. You are
a legend, the little girl conquering the ocean.

The tides of your girlhood shape the shores
of your knowing. Your daughters question why

you exhaust yourself with worry, ceding to
concern. Sea salt polished your toddler face.

You bite your nails. Your daughters catch
a whiff of salt seething from your tonsils. You,

puzzled by the wilds before you, you do not
realize that you are already doing the unimaginable,

raising one girl after another. The eldest is a siren
bearing your name. Your daughters beach whales

and conjure clouds. Your daughters are the work
you are forced to do and your desires for sons

swell. You abandon your daughters in expan-
sive anxieties. You're obsessed with sons, tread

the tears of King Henry's wanton wives. You
see fate as a buoy, cradling flesh. Your body

is an unwavering presence before your husband.
Your daughters resent lighthouses, welcome

tempests. Your daughters long to know you, sand
stinging in their eyes. You want to reinvent yourself,

chasing raindrops with your tongue, trying to be enough
for someone's grown son, baiting the heavens for a boy.

NEW YEAR'S DAY 2021

There are Black girls in America and everywhere.

There are Black girls from America in Haiti, Mauritius, Bangladesh, Burma, China, Japan, Kenya, El Salvador, Canada, the North Pole, Iceland, South Africa, Samoa, Australia, New Zealand, the Netherlands, Singapore, Cyprus, Germany, Malesia, Cambodia, Brazil, Venezuela, Kenya, Israel, Turkey, Saudi Arabia, Denmark, India, and everywhere.

There are Black girls from Haiti, Mauritius, Bangladesh, Burma, China, Japan, Kenya, El Salvador, Canada, the North Pole, Iceland, Tanzania, South Africa, Australia, New Zealand, the Netherlands, Singapore, Germany, Malesia, Cambodia, Brazil, Venezuela, Uruguay, Kenya, Israel, Zambia, Turkey, Saudi Arabia, India, and everywhere in America.

There are Black girls in America in cages. And everywhere?

There are Black girls from Haiti, Mauritius, Bangladesh, Burma, China, Japan, Kenya, El Salvador, Canada, Yemen, the North Pole, Iceland, South Africa, Australia, New Zealand, the Netherlands, Singapore, Germany, Trinidad and Tobago, Malesia, Cambodia, Brazil, Venezuela, Kenya, Israel, Turkey, Saudi Arabia, India, Poland, and everywhere in America in cages. And dying?

There are people who like it this way. They hold the locks and chains. These people are us. They are chain-fence-linked arm in arm with bystanders. These people are also us.

#BRINGBACKOURGIRLS—NOT A STORY

This is not a story, but old as creation, dark as the Middle Ages, dark as the dawn of the European Renaissance, dark as the discovery of new worlds, dark as the gold-covered-in-espresso stains of first menses, dark as the most beautiful Sudanese princess, dark as the oil out of the Middle East, dark as diamond mines outside Cape Town, dark as us, the bark of ancient trees on the sea islands of South Carolina, dark as those who still call themselves marooned on the Canary Islands, dark as the cimarrons in the mountains of Colombia, as those who hid in the Great Dismal Swamp, dark as Haitian mambo mothers spitting tobacco in the faces of gentile men tearing at their skirts, dark as the heart of war in the name of wealth, dark as the coldest day in winter, dark as the shadows of the northern lights, dark as a cobra's skin and the venom pulsing, dark as the nostril of a caged bird through the eyes of a snake, dark as the heart of a man who would tell a nation to shoot Lysol into their veins like dope, dark like greedy men who tell you that your grandparents want to die for you, because they want you to be a customer zombie gliding through the dark of Walmart, dark and hard as the pavement where Jill Nelson wrote TRUMP=PLAGUE in chalk to save our dusking lives, dark as self-induced ignorance, dark as any, dark as our decency fermenting and rotting in instant grits, dark as the insides of our bellies as we sit here wondering and well removed from the violence of two hundred girls being ripped from their chairs, torn out of physics exams and tossed into trucks stained in blood and the grit of gunpower. Dark and heavy as the otherness, dark as the doors of a bank vault underground. Dark and heavy as the stillness of this page. And who among us would have the courage to run? Dark as the birthing closets where *ianfu* keep life's secrets that splint the economies of empires, rape has always been a war strategy, has always been a broken soldier's reward. Dark as the ore mined to make the nickel you will use to buy this book, dark as the ink of the contract used to bind this book. Dark as my rage about these children, my heavenly hosts of girl-children—stolen and sold to swell the pockets of greedy men, with hearts black enough to be poisoned with nostalgia. They want for the days when human flesh was flashy currency.

#BRINGBACKOURGIRLS—PREMONITION ONE

More than one felt the chill
in her bones. Counting 276
ixora blooms scattered in front
of a bar, you, the youngest,
eager to become a woman, think
these petals are blood, crimson
oil rounding in the grooves
of your fingerprints, perfumed
violets and coffee berries.
Any living thing on the fringe
of the danger remains beautiful.
The chaos of bait, the anticipation
before the bite. You are smart enough
to know torn rose petals in the road
are clear signs of rejection, blasphemy
against beauty.

You remember the side-striped jackal,
he stands soft as a tallow tree
on the edge, randy as a hyena, wicked
as a Westerner. You have forgotten him,
a wanderer with a sweet tooth. He has
heard about England's shepherd's pies.
His cravings are made of wishes and
wilderness. For him, collecting a wound
is easy work. Ask any jackal whose neck

is rubbed raw from a leash. This kind
of working man wants a wife who can
mend, put care into the carved-out
spaces. He wants a woman for
his wound, crisscrossing the stiches
sideways, looping the lattice that
dresses him where he is not whole.
He wants your soft hand to hold in
his crimson oils.

#BRINGBACKOURGIRLS—PREMONITION TWO

In a dream a pencil marches
onto the back of a truck;
the grin of a girl erased
in the face of a war. You are
in a nightmare. The boy in your
ear has forgotten the face
of his mother. The soldier knows
her smell. He doesn't know
his sisters. He doesn't know
that you dream and negotiate
even in your nightmares. He doesn't
know you risk flying and won't eat
death or any unwanted duties. He has
counted forty-eight of you, schoolgirls
with lead on your tongues, smudged
into your nail beds. Many of you leap
into the sky from the back of a truck,
molded from iron cages.

#BRINGBACKOURGIRLS—WHO IS CRIMINAL?

Old men decided your vanishing
was a theft. They did not call
you comfort women, prisoners
of war capable of collecting
reparations for the pricelessness
of your body, your life. This
is what I know. Your elected allies
think less of you than your captors.
Collectively, your allies and your
captors, they will blame your vanishing
on some holy war, but they will not use
the story of Elijah taking to wind, or
the one about rolling away the stones.
They will make sure all understand
that oppression is righteous, ordained by
the lords. They want us to see you
as if you were dolls abandoned
in a secondhand shop. The ones meant
to be left out of the toy box. They call
you daughters—under the breath. Fathers
weep, mothers hunt soldiers with baby rattles
and machetes. A mother knows the labyrinth
of diplomacy like the lines in your hand.
What man would sacrifice his "wife"
for a commander and not be
criminal?

#BRINGBACKOURGIRLS—
PREMONITION THREE

Before the rocket's red glare
over oceans and Pearl Harbor,
generations' worth of Korean girls
were tossed from chairs and desks,
taken from schools and thrown
into brothels. There, 1 soldier,
sometimes 5, sometimes 60,
uses your body to dress the wounds
not decorated with his blood. A Korean
girl, you will not stop running. Doctors
half your age will diagnose you with sleepwalking.
Tell you it is dangerous for your mind
to list the names when your heart wishes
them the worst deaths. You shut your eyes.

Daughters rock themselves when
they hear grandmothers snoring,
see grandmothers kicking at the air, swinging
canes into the houseplants, before they
go tender into their quilts. There is
always one left to recount the tales, else,
a war and its ways may have never
really ever happened. The tree
dropping in a forest far away, let's
say Nigeria, let's say Borno, without
anyone around to hear is a kind
of mystery.

#BRINGBACKOURGIRLS—
PREMONITION FOUR

The 2015 man is the mirror of the 1944
man. They resemble. Maybe 2015 is the great
nephew of the Imperial Commander, a Japanese
man says "only 20,000 women" slushed beneath
cold men and ordered to love. Imperial soldiers
in wheelchairs pick at their scars, reciting
the nicknames of ghosts, recalling the men
they murdered. One soldier sobs. Proof
screams in ink and 5 witnesses turn into 410,000
women. Together you become a wave of warm
bodies beneath a tsunami of Imperial uniforms.

Memory fires, a grenade lands, dams break. You
cry so loud your sisters are sure you are bleeding
beneath a man wanting to love you, but left love in
the rice-field battles. The world is at war with itself.
Many are made to be comfort women, cauls over their
faces, a gauze. You are the women wading in wastelands,
vast like oceans, deep like generations in Korea,
in China, in the Philippines, in Burma, in Thailand,
in Taiwan, in Malaysia, in Vietnam, in New Orleans,
in Port-au-Prince, in Rio de Janeiro, in
Havana, in Miami, in Atlanta, in Lagos,
in Luanda, in Porto-Novo, in Yaoundé,
in Praia, in Las Vegas, in Los Angeles,
in Brazzaville, in Accra, in Guinea-Bissau, in

Girl. Photo by Anna K. Stone. annakstone.com.

Monrovia, in Malia, in Dakar, in Freetown,
in Juba, in New York, in Rome, in the District
of Columbia, in Paris, in Berlin, in the cobblestoned
trenches of London, and in every millimeter
of the Vatican, needless to say in Florence,
in Cirò, in Lexington, Kentucky, even in
the shipping crates in the Port of Baltimore,
and at the piers of Hong Kong, in the holocaust,
the one in Germany and the one of the Atlantic
skirting the Americas.

Diplomats want to comfort you. Women,
lost souls, will tell you about
girls, brilliant as suns, their minds cast rays
from their eyes and ears. Their pencils are
emblazoned in a physics lab at an exam
that will make them fit to fill wounds.
Medical school will make each a doctor,
who erases AIDS from the breasts of mothers
and the mounds of flesh that form a lover.

#BRINGBACKOURGIRLS— WAIFS AND WANTING

Waifs have been taught by their gods
Western + education (girls) = prostitute.
Waifs fling you from your desks like
lice. Set fire to your toes. To make
a wife from a schoolgirl, waifs rob
you, rustle your first life into a ball.
Make school a memory. Make
you forget your mother, your first
teacher. Make you a wife of war. Bruise
your face. Ringing clots into your wrists.
Stripes, gashes, at your knees. Making
you devout. Make you beg forgiveness
for not being the woman he wants, for not
being rich, for not being broad on your
back and long in your legs. He may be
too short to have tall and strong sons
to live the dreams towering over him.

#BRINGBACKOURGIRLS—MAMA'S BOY?

Every wife must apologize for not being her husband's
mother? But he will not forgive you. The absence
of his mother's kiss is the scar of repeated
wounding. He marries you too young, before
he littered his seeds along the road. This is why
he can't get a young wife from the market. You
have used him up and witched him, made him old
in all the wrong places.

You have cursed him. Made his beer warm
too quick, made the bottle too slippy, too hard
for him to hold on. You make his head lop-
sided. Make the beer miss his lips. His shirt
gulps the beer instead. It is all you. You make him
smell like piss in his brother's yard. You leave him
without choices. It is because of you.
His knees don't work. He will not let you heal
his wounds. You wanted to be a doctor, so you must
have wished him crippled in all these ways. No
glory for a man who enters war wounded.

* * *

(for my niece and her bullies)

when they come for you,
know they will be creeping,
silence and secrets are weapons—
cry out.
the sacred names
in contralto harmonies.
breathe centuries of terror,
your melodic shrills
will shield you in Mahakali
and will summon
Dahomey warriors.

when they come for you,
know their lips will itch.
they will hunger to kiss.
bite them.
let the whites of your eyes
curse.
they will be blinded by our chariots
in your glares.

when they come for you,
know they will offer worms
from their guts.
kick them.
invert their assumptions

A mother and daughter kneel at a protest of the death of George Floyd (2020). AP Photo/Jacquelyn Martin.

use your power
they will want to beat you
we will sever hands,
and give their bodies
over to dust.

when they come for you
they will threaten you lonely
remember
our sacred names
the sharpness
under your lips

Piercing your enemies, beckoning
generations of blood. We will give you
a red canal to cart your joy. This will be
your carpet. You are our vanity wading
in their envy.

You, our calypso,
you are our headwater.
We will come.
Dahomey, Mahakali,
black, blue-winged avengers. We
are your angel armies. We
will come, charging in
your veins armed with stars.
Remember that even your toes
are heaven bound.

ACKNOWLEDGMENTS

This book would not exist without a community of Black girls—some infant, some grown, some granny, and some levitating in between. I recognize the God in you. Thank you to my sisters, blood-related and designated, for being the air I breathe. I recognize the God in you. Dear friends, thank you for holding my hand as I walk this journey and the next. I recognize the God in you. I am also grateful to the ancestors, generations, and future Black girls—those who are not yet born, but are already loved. I recognize the God in you. I belong to you; you belong to me.

Thank you to the Wintergreen women, the minis (mentees), the MEGAS (mentors), the church ladies, the educational aunties, the sister writers/scholars/artists/archivists, and the midwives of the re/evolution. I also want to acknowledge and thank all the Jersey girls and divas who can write, sing, act, dance, create, and wrestle your hearts from the concrete on command. Your presence is everywhere. Your names are far too many to list…I recognize the God in you. I belong to you; you belong to me.

Thank you to all the Black girl guardians and the fellas on the front lines for Black girl liberation—my father, my brothers-nephews-uncles-cousins-family, my friends, those play brothers, those brother writers/scholars/artists/archivists, the young and the old lovers, and those who love tender as rainbows and cackle with me in bright colors. I also want to thank my son for choosing this Black girl to be his mother and loving me in my wholeness and complexity. I recognize the God in you. I belong to you; you belong to me.

I give special thanks to the institutions that are doing the work to nurture and narrate the lives of Black girls, specifically the Saving Our Lives, Hearing Our Truths collective, the Urban Bush Women, the "Giggles, Guts, and Glitter" clique, and The Colored Girls Museum, founded by the visionary genius Vashti DuBois. Thank you to Charlotte Sheedy and everyone at Sheedy Literary Agency for always supporting my vision. Thank you to Nancy Miller and everyone at Bloomsbury Publishing/Macmillan Publishers for bringing this vision to print. I recognize God in the work you do. I acknowledge the blessing that you are. I belong to you; you belong to me.

I am grateful for the support of the Furious Flower Poetry Center at James Madison University; MacDowell; the Watering Hole Poetry Org; the Kentucky Foundation for Women; Vermont Studio Center; Bread Loaf Writers' Conference for Poetry; the Commonwealth Institute for Black Studies, the Arts and Sciences Dean's Office, and the Office for the Vice President for Research at the University of Kentucky; the Project on the History of Black Writing at the University of Kansas; the Center for Black Literature at Medgar Evers College; the Institute of African American Affairs and the Center for Black Visual Culture at New York University; the Gordon Parks Foundation; the New York Public Library; the Poets and Scholars Summer Writing Workshop at the Institute for the Study of Global Racial Justice at Rutgers University; and others. I recognize God in the work you do. I acknowledge the blessing that you are. I belong to you; you belong to me.

I also want to thank God in all her many forms, the past lives, and the yet-to-be, without you this book would not be possible. I belong to you; you belong to me.

CITATIONS

Bambara, Toni Cade. *Gorilla, My Love*. New York: Knopf Doubleday Publishing Group, 2011. Ebook.

Brooks, Gwendolyn. *In the Mecca: Poems*. New York: Harper & Row, 1968.

Brown, Ruth Nicole. *Black Girlhood Celebration: Toward a Hip-Hop Feminist Pedagogy*. New York: Peter Lang, 2009.

Clifton, Lucille. *Good Woman: Poems and a Memoir 1969–1980*. Rochester, NY: BOA Editions Limited, 2014.

Crenshaw, Kimberlé Williams, with Priscilla Ocen and Jyoti Nanda. *Black Girls Matter: Pushed Out, Overpoliced and Underprotected*. African American Policy Forum and Center for Intersectionality and Social Policy Studies. 2015. Accessed July 2, 2021. https://44bbdc6e -01a4-4a9a-88bc-731c6524888e.filesusr.com/ugd/ 62e126_4011b574b92145e383234513a24ad15a.pdf.

Finney, Nikky. *Love Child's Hotbed of Occasional Poetry: Poems & Artifacts*. Evanston, IL: TriQuarterly Books/Northwestern University Press, 2020.

Fleetwood, Nicole R. *Marking Time: Art in the Age of Incarceration*. Cambridge, MA: Harvard University Press, 2020.

Gabbin, Joanne Veal, ed. *Shaping Memories: Reflections of African American Women Writers*. Jackson: University Press of Mississippi, 2009.

García Márquez, Gabriel. *One Hundred Years of Solitude*. Trans. Gregory Rabassa. London: Penguin Classics, 2000.\

Halliday, Aria. "Black Girls' Feistiness as Everyday Resistance in Toni Cade Bambara's *Gorilla, My Love*." *Palimpsest* 9, no. 1 (2020): 50–64.

Hartman, Saidiya V. *Wayward Lives, Beautiful Experiments: Intimate Histories of Social Upheaval*. New York: W. W. Norton, 2019.

Hurston, Zora Neale, and Robert Hemenway. *Dust Tracks on a Road: An Autobiography*. New York: HarperCollins, 2006.

Jordan, June. *Technical Difficulties: African-American Notes on the State of the Union*. New York: Pantheon Books, 1992.

Morris, Monique W. *Pushout: The Criminalization of Black Girls in Schools*. New York: New Press, 2016.

Nelson, Marilyn, Elizabeth Alexander, and Floyd Cooper. *Miss Crandall's School for Young Ladies and Little Misses of Color: Poems*. Honesdale, PA: Wordsong, 2007.

Perry, Imani. *Breathe: A Letter to My Sons*. Boston: Beacon Press, 2019.

Perry, Imani. *More Beautiful and More Terrible: The Embrace and Transcendence of Racial Inequality in the United States*. New York: New York University Press, 2011.

Smith, Patricia. *Shoulda Been Jimi Savannah*. Minneapolis: Coffee House Press, 2013.

Trethewey, Natasha. *Memorial Drive: A Daughter's Memoir*. New York: Ecco, 2020.

Whaley, Deborah Elizabeth. *Black Women in Sequence: Re-inking Comics, Graphic Novels, and Anime*. Seattle: University of Washington Press, 2015.

Wright, Nazera Sadiq. *Black Girlhood in the Nineteenth Century*. Urbana: University of Illinois Press, 2016.

PHOTO CREDITS

p. xxiii: Schomburg Center for Research in Black Culture, Jean Blackwell Hutson Research and Reference Division, The New York Public Library. "Hoe work." New York Public Library Digital Collections. Photo by Dorothea Lange, 1940. https://digitalcollections.nypl.org/items/510d47e4-746a-a3d9-e040-e00a18064a99

p. 2: Schomburg Center for Research in Black Culture, Jean Blackwell Hutson Research and Reference Division, The New York Public Library. "Group of Phyllis Wheatley Girls." New York Public Library Digital Collections, 1922. https://digitalcollections.nypl.org/items/510d47dd-ec12-a3d9-e040-e00a18064a99

p. 6: Schomburg Center for Research in Black Culture, Jean Blackwell Hutson Research and Reference Division, The New York Public Library. "Little Blanche Taylor. Franklin, Ky.; Rev. T.W. Haigler." New York Public Library Digital Collections, 1907. https://digitalcollections.nypl.org/items/510d47df-a05d-a3d9-e040-e00a18064a99

p. 8: Gilbert Studios, Washington, D.C. (C. M. Gilbert), 1894; restored by Adam Cuerden [public domain], via Wikimedia Commons. https://commons.wikimedia.org/w/index.php?title=File:Gilbert_Studios_photograph_of_Harriet_Jacobs.jpg&oldid=575734440

p. 11: Vintage property of ullstein bild, 1903. Photo by ulstein bild via Getty Images

p. 12: Schomburg Center for Research in Black Culture, Photographs and Prints Division, The New York Public Library. "Children of defense worker; Negro slum district, Norfolk,Va., Mar. 1940." New York Public Library Digital Collections. Photo by John Vachon, 1940. https://digitalcollections.nypl.org/items/510d47df-f906-a3d9-e040-e00a18064a99

p. 15: Schomburg Center for Research in Black Culture, Jean Blackwell Hutson Research and Reference Division, The New York Public Library. "African American girls playing games." New York Public Library Digital Collections, 1922. https://digitalcollections.nypl.org/items/510d47df-9509-a3d9-e040-e00a18064a99

p. 16: "'It Ain't Gonna Be Me' Recording Session," Detroit, MI, 1989. Photo by Michael Ochs Archives/Getty Images

p. 22: "Recording of Aretha Franklin's Album 'This Girl's in Love with You' At Atlantic Studios," New York, NY, 1969. Photo by Stephen Paley/Michael Ochs Archives/Getty Images

p. 25: "Queen Of Soul Recording," New York, NY, January 9, 1969. Photo by Michael Ochs Archives/Getty Images

p. 26: "Aretha Franklin," 1968. Photo by Express Newspapers/Getty Images

p. 30: "Queen Of Soul Holding Her 'Soul '69' Album," New York, NY, January 9, 1969. Photo by Michael Ochs Archives/Getty Images

p. 33: Photo courtesy of the author

p. 36: Schomburg Center for Research in Black Culture, Jean Blackwell Hutson Research and Reference Division, The New York Public Library. "What is home without me." New York Public Library Digital Collections, 1914. https://digitalcollections.nypl.org/items/510d47df-9dd2-a3d9-e040-e00a18064a99

p. 38: "Young Girl Laughing," Chicago, IL, 1973. Image courtesy National Archives. Photo via Smith Collection/Gado/Getty Images

p. 40: "Whitney Houston," February 1982. Photo by Jack Mitchell/Getty Images

p. 44: Photo by Kyna Uwaeme

p. 48: Photo courtesy of the author

p. 53: "Young Whitney Houston Portrait Sessions," West Orange, NJ, c. 1982. Photo by Bette Marshall/Getty Images

p. 54: Schomburg Center for Research in Black Culture, Jean Blackwell Hutson Research and Reference Division, The New York Public Library. "Girl reserves." New York Public Library Digital Collections, 1919. https://digitalcollections.nypl.org/items/510d47de-1d45-a3d9-e040-e00a18064a99

p. 60: "Queen Latifah Live in Concert," Gary, IN, February 1990. Photo by Raymond Boyd/Getty Images

p. 73: Photo by Anna K. Stone. annakstone.com

p. 78: Photo by Anna K. Stone. annakstone.com

p. 79: *Outside Looking In*, Mobile, AL, 1956. The Gordon Parks Foundation

p. 82: "Little Girl Outside Grocery in Mississippi," 1996. Photo by Shepard Sherbell/Corbis via Getty Images

p. 88: Photo by Arden Barnes

p. 101: "King Speaks," Montgomery, AL, 1956. Photo by Michael Ochs Archives/Getty Images

p. 117: "Urban Bush Women." Photo by Hayim Heron

p. 133: Photo by Anna K. Stone. annakstone.com

p. 138: AP Photo/Jacquelyn Martin

A NOTE ON THE AUTHOR

DaMaris B. Hill, PhD, is the author of *A Bound Woman Is a Dangerous Thing: The Incarceration of African American Women from Harriet Tubman to Sandra Bland* (2020 NAACP Image Award nominee for Outstanding Literary Work in Poetry), *The Fluid Boundaries of Suffrage and Jim Crow: Staking Claims in the American Heartland,* and \Vi-zə-bəl\ \Teks-chərs\ (*Visible Textures*). She has a keen interest in the work of Toni Morrison and theories regarding "rememory" as a philosophy and aesthetic practice. Hill has studied with writers such as Lucille Clifton, Monifa Love Asante, Natasha Trethewey, Nikky Finney, David Rivard, Deborah Willis, and others. Her development as a writer has also been enhanced by the institutional support of MacDowell, Vermont Studio Center, Bread Loaf Writers' Conference, Key West Literary Seminar/Writers' Workshop Program, *Callaloo* Creative Writing Workshop, the Institute for Digital Research in the Humanities, the Project on the History of Black Writing, the Watering Hole Poetry Org, the Furious Flower Poetry Center, and others. Similarly to her creative process, Hill's scholarly research is interdisciplinary. Hill is an associate professor of creative writing at the University of Kentucky.

damarishill.com

4/22